THE TASTE OF AFRICA

THE UNDISCOVERED FOOD & COOKING OF AN EXTRAORDINARY CONTINENT

A journey through the culinary history, traditions and ingredients of Africa in 80 mouthwatering recipes and over 370 step-by-step photographs

Rosamund Grant and Josephine Bacon

southwater

This edition is published by Southwater,
an imprint of Anness Publishing Ltd
Hermes House, 88–89 Blackfriars Road, London SE1 8HA
tel. 020 7401 2077; fax 020 7633 9499
www.southwaterbooks.com; www.annesspublishing.com

If you like the images in this book and would like to investigate using
them for publishing, promotions or advertising, please visit our website
www.practicalpictures.com for more information.

UK agent: The Manning Partnership Ltd: tel. 01225 478444;
fax 01225 478440; sales@manning-partnership.co.uk
UK distributor: Grantham Book Services Ltd: tel. 01476 541080;
fax 01476 541061; orders@gbs.tbs-ltd.co.uk
North American agent/distributor: National Book Network
tel. 301 459 3366; fax 301 429 5746; www.nbnbooks.com
Australian agent/distributor: Pan Macmillan Australia
tel. 1300 135 113; fax 1300 135 103;
customer.service@macmillan.com.au
New Zealand agent/distributor: David Bateman Ltd
tel. (09) 415 7664; fax (09) 415 8892

Publisher: Joanna Lorenz
Editorial Director: Helen Sudell
Editors: Joanne Rippin and Elizabeth Woodland
Photographs: Craig Robertson, William Adams-Lingwood,
Patrick McLeavey and Martin Brigdale
Recipes: Ghillie Basan, Rosamund Grant, Rebekah Hassan
and Soheila Kimberley
Designer: Adelle Morris
Cover Designer: Balley Design Associates
Production Controller: Wendy Lawson

The Publishers would like to thank the following picture libraries for
the use of their images: Corbis pp 7, 8b, 11 all, 12 all, 13, 14b;
Travel Ink pp 8t, 9, 10, 14t, 15t.

ETHICAL TRADING POLICY: Because of our ongoing ecological
investment programme, you, as our customer, can have the pleasure
and reassurance of knowing that a tree is being cultivated on your
behalf to naturally replace the materials used to make the book you are
holding. For further information about this scheme, go to
www.annesspublishing.com/trees

© Anness Publishing Ltd 2008, 2009

Previously published as part of a larger volume, *Food and Cooking of Africa and
the Middle East*

NOTES: Bracketed terms are intended for American readers.
For all recipes, quantities are given in both metric and imperial
measures, and, where appropriate, measures are also given in
standard cups and spoons. Follow one set, but not a mixture, because
they are not interchangeable. Standard spoon and cup measures are level.
1 tsp = 5ml, 1 tbsp = 15 ml, 1 cup = 250ml/8fl oz.
Australian standard tablespoons are 20ml. Australian readers should
use 3 tsp in place of 1 tbsp for measuring small quantities of gelatine,
flour, salt, etc.
American pints are 16fl oz/2 cups. American readers should use
20fl oz/2.5 cups in place of 1 pint when measuring liquids.
Electric oven temperatures in this book are for conventional ovens. When using a
fan oven, the temperature will probably need to be reduced by about
10–20°C/20–40°F. Since ovens vary, you should check with your manufacturer's
instruction book for guidance.
The nutritional analysis given for each recipe is calculated per portion
(i.e. serving or item), unless otherwise stated. If the recipe gives a range, such as
Serves 4–6, then the nutritional analysis will be for the smaller portion size, i.e. 6
servings. Measurements for sodium do not include salt added to taste. Medium
(US large) eggs are used unless otherwise stated.

PUBLISHER'S NOTE: Although the advice and information in this book are
believed to be accurate and true at the time of going to press, neither the authors
nor the publisher can accept any legal responsibility or liability for any errors or
omissions that may be made nor for any inaccuracies nor for any harm or injury
that comes about from following instructions or advice in this book.

CONTENTS

INTRODUCTION

Eating today is an adventure in taste and discovery as we explore other cuisines and cultures through the food we enjoy. Africa is a vast area that has introduced a wide range of exciting flavours for us to discover. Many of their recipes are familiar to us, but there are still many more that are less well known. In this book we take a journey through this varied cuisine.

The huge continent of Africa embraces many countries with their diverse cultures and widely differing climates. Many foods are indigenous to Africa, such as okra and melons, but many others were introduced over the centuries, and some have arrived by natural means – birds and strong sea currents. Visitors to the continent from ancient times as well as traders and colonists over the last 500 years brought their culinary heritage with them and this became absorbed into some parts of African culture. Those visitors also adapted traditional African meals to suit their own palates and took them back to their own countries.

African cooks inherit their cooking techniques by word of mouth and then develop their skills by experimenting with different ingredients and cooking methods. The resulting creations are new and interesting and it would be true to say that they cook from the heart. Dishes include staples such as rice, yams and cassava, combined with hot peppery stews, or beans, lentils, nuts, a variety of vegetables and perhaps some meat, fish or poultry.

Along part of Africa's Mediterranean coast are the countries of the Maghreb, which are Algeria, Morocco and Tunisia. Here we will find a distinctive cuisine using exotic spice mixtures, fresh seafood, and couscous mixed with brightly coloured vegetables and sometimes fruit. The tagine is a traditional North African method of slow cooking using a tall funnelled pot, which gives succulent results.

Left: Chickpea Tagine, a popular North African dish, in the pot that gives the dish its name, and Egusi, Spinach and Egg in the foreground.

Throughout Africa, vegetable, bean and lentil dishes are extremely popular, whereas meat, poulty, fish and shellfish are often used merely as one of a number of flavourings, rather than as the main ingredients. In West Africa, spicy tomato-based sauces are very well-liked, while in the east of the continent, the influence of Indian cooking on the traditional African cuisine makes for an interesting and delicious culinary adventure.

Eating in Africa is a unique and exciting experience. Throughout the continent cooks use the same or similar ingredients, but often prepare and cook them in different ways according to local tradition and custom. For example, in some West African countries okra is chopped very finely, until it is reduced almost to a pulp, giving a rich silky consistency to sauces and soups, while elsewhere the okra is often left whole to give a completely different result.

The essential staples – yams, cassava, green bananas and plantains – are used throughout Africa, either on their own or combined with others to make Fu Fu, a popular accompaniment to all sorts of savoury dishes.

Sweet potatoes, coconuts, okra, a huge variety of green vegetables, beans and pulses, nuts, and grains, such as corn, are all common cooking ingredients, while all sorts of wonderful, tropical fruits, such as mangoes, avocados and paw paw, are a familiar sight and are eaten at any time of the day – not just reserved for dessert.

Bringing together the authentic cooking style and classic foodstuffs of this vast diverse region, this book creates a colourful and enticing resource of recipes which share origins, ingredients and influences. An extensive introduction details the countries covered, their different cooking traditions and ingredients. The following four chapters provide dishes that range from soups, appetizers and snacks, main courses, vegetarian dishes, salads and accompaniments to delectable pastries and desserts.

Join us in a culinary tour of this exciting land, as you discover some of the varied and enticing dishes that make up the food and cooking of Africa.

Below: A busy market stall selling different types of grain in Abuja, Nigeria.

THE AFRICAN CONTINENT

Africa can be divided into three principal areas, both geographically and from a culinary point of view: North Africa, sub-Saharan Africa and the expanse of southern Africa.

NORTH AFRICA

This area is itself divided into the narrow, fertile coastal strip along the Mediterranean and on either side of the Nile, which was the hub of the ancient world, and the desert. Typically Mediterranean produce – olives, grapes, figs, dates, pomegranates and almonds – are enjoyed in the fertile areas of the north, and rich creamy milk and dairy products are provided by water buffalo in the well-watered areas. Flocks of sheep and goats that feed on the sparse vegetation of the Saharan hinterland provide most of the meat in the diet.

Egypt

The cuisine in Egypt is very similar to that of its Middle Eastern neighbours. Many dishes are made with legumes – lentils, beans and chickpeas – including two of the national dishes, ful medames and falafel. Rice and cracked wheat are both staples. Okra, that most pan-African of vegetables, is used to thicken soups and stews, as is *meloukhia*, a

Above: Men in a rowing-boat, and in a dhow in the background, use traditional methods to catch fish in the River Nile.

bright green, spinach-like leaf. *Meloukhia* soup is a universally popular dish that may be made with the fresh leaf when in season, or with dried, powdered *meloukhia*. Because most of the population is crowded between large stretches of water – the Mediterranean and the Nile – fish are of prime importance. Tilapia flourish in the brackish waters of the Great Bitter Lake, now part of the Suez Canal, where they are also farmed. Sardines, red and grey mullet and tuna are among the fish caught in the Mediterranean. Nile perch are the favourite freshwater fish.

The Maghreb

The cuisine of the three countries of the Maghreb – Algeria, Morocco and Tunisia – is distinctive, ranging from highly sophisticated in the towns to basic in the countryside, the Atlas Mountains and the desert. Magical spice mixtures are typical of the Maghreb, including ras al hanout, in which ground cumin and hot red pepper from the Sudan, known as *filfil soudani*, predominate.

The staple of these countries is couscous, made from durum (hard) wheat or semolina. The grains are soaked in hot water and separated individually by hand, while being evenly coated with smen – clarified butter – by continuous rubbing. This is a long and monotonous task that can take up to eight hours. It is a common sight in a North African village to see women sitting outside their front doors, a large metal bowl of couscous on their knees, as they chat to their neighbours while

Left: A herd of the distinctive cattle of the Dinka people graze on the fertile lands of the Massai Mara in Kenya.

endlessly performing the lifting and rubbing movement to separate and soften the grains. In the towns, the packets of ready-made couscous – couscous *tout prêt* – show that fast food has penetrated even here, and making couscous is now a matter of minutes, rather than hours. Morocco is also famous for its *warka*, a thin dough similar to filo that is made into pies and pastries, in particular Bistilla, the famous pigeon pie. In Tunisia, the same dough is called *brik*.

THE SAHARA

The vast white expanse on the map below the countries of North Africa, and encroaching into their boundaries, is the Sahara: the world's largest desert, which can easily be seen from outer space. Here, existence has always been at subsistence level; food is hoarded and diets are meagre.

SUB-SAHARAN AFRICA

The countries of Senegal, Mali, Niger and Chad are all former French colonies, so traces of French culture remain, especially in the more fertile Senegal. The Sahara gives way here to the Sahel, a semi-arid plain where rainfall is still too low to produce crops. Protein here has added importance, but the inhabitants subsist on imported food and fermented milk, smen and dried fish from the coasts. Meat is a luxury food, eaten during festivals in the form of *mechoui*: spit-roasted lamb or goat, stuffed with rice and vegetables. Dried tomatoes and aubergines (eggplants) enliven the diets in these countries, and they are also available in Libya and, in the north the Sudan.

Despite the dryness, the countries of the Horn of Africa – eastern Sudan, Ethiopia, Somalia and the tiny state of Djibouti – have their own treasure: coffee, which is drunk at high strength. Ethiopians roast the dried, greenish beans only when they are about to drink them. The freshly roasted beans are then ground down as finely as possible and boiled in water to form the thick, syrupy drink that is familiar throughout North Africa and the Middle East.

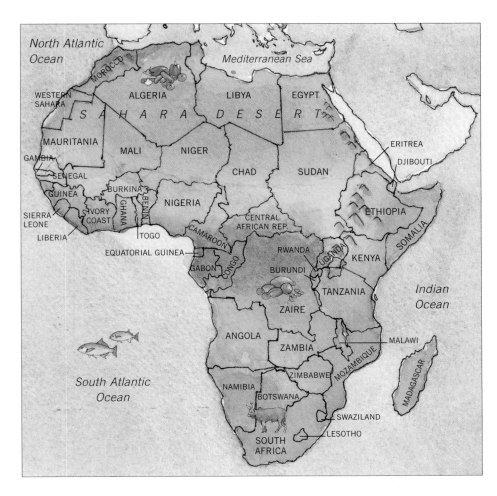

Although Ethiopians eat rice, they also have their own distinctive bread, which is made not from wheat but from a millet-like grain called teff. Unlike the tough flat breads of the Touareg and other nomads, Ethiopian bread, known as *injera*, is soft and pliable, made with a very liquid yeasty dough. It looks rather like terry towelling and has a very sour flavour because it has been leavened with wild yeasts. It is used to mop up the fiery sauces that accompany Ethiopian meat and vegetable stews.

West and Central Africa

Below the Sahara lie the thick rainforest areas of West and Central Africa, with their steamy heat, and where it is said that if you plant a stick in the ground it will take root and bear leaves like the biblical Aaron's rod. The staples here are mealies, corn cobs and cassava root, and similar large fleshy roots such as eddoes and cocoyams (colocasia). There is a profusion of vegetables, dominated by okra, squashes and beans. Most of the animal protein is in the form of fish from inland and coastal waters, as meat is in short supply.

Southern Africa

The terrain that makes up the south of Africa is a patchwork of deserts and fertile land, on which the European settlers established a strong farming tradition, allowing more intensive and productive agriculture, with pasture for cattle to graze on.

In South Africa there are strong differences between the diet of native peoples in the bush and the town-dwellers, black and white. The South Africans have developed their own distinctive foods, including dried meats – biltong – and sausages – *boerewors* – and *boboties*, a mixture of ground meat and spices.

THE AFRICAN KITCHEN

Food is scarce and precious in some areas of Africa, particularly the arid regions, and meat is rarely eaten. Dried and preserved foods are important elements in the diet, with fresh fish available only on the coast and from areas with lakes and rivers. Grains – rice, barley, wheat, maize, millet and *acha* – as well as dried beans are the backbone of the diet throughout Africa.

TRADITIONS PASSED DOWN

The North African kitchen is a sophisticated one, whose traditions date back thousands of years and whose recipes have been recorded in Arabic down through the centuries. Only in North Africa are so many cooking techniques used. Throughout the rest of the continent recipes are handed down from mother to daughter, and rarely written down. Measurements are flexible, and are usually made by handfuls, cups, calabashes and old tins, in particular Players cigarette tins, which are used in the tropics.

Throughout Africa cooking is performed almost exclusively by women, and in sub-Sarahan and southern regions the cooking techniques are slow and sometimes laborious. The pounding of mealies and yams, the fluffing of couscous grains, the peeling and shelling of beans and peas, the trimming of vegetables, the preparation of aromatic stews – these are all tasks that the average African girl learns from her mother from an early age.

Cassava, which originates from South America, contains quantities of hydrocyanic acid, making it too poisonous to be simply peeled and boiled, like a potato. In West and East Africa, it is cooked and then pounded to ensure that the acid evaporates. The sight of village women pounding cassava, using a huge pestle in a decorative wooden mortar, has been a familiar one for centuries.

Pounded yams are called *foufou*, which has a consistency similar to that of couscous. *Foufou* is a staple food of Nigeria. Rice is also an important staple, and Jollof Rice can be considered the Nigerian national dish.

Above: Women in Kenya pound cassava with a pestle in a mortar to release the poisonous hydrocyanic acid.

FOREIGN INFLUENCES

Africa has been subject to several foreign influences throughout the centuries, and this is reflected in its regional cuisine. In West Africa, it was traders – and eventually slavers – from western Europe, especially Portugal and England, and later those from the Americas, who traded with the Ashanti Empire, with its huge wealth of gold and diamonds. It is surprising how many of the African staple foods actually derive from elsewhere. Many, such as cassava, coconut, pomegranates and bananas, were brought in trading ships carried on the strong currents that run through the Indian and Atlantic Oceans between India and Africa or South America and Africa. The Arabs were early traders, bringing many spices with them, especially to East Africa.

One example of a staple ingredient introduced from outside the continent is the opuntia cactus, known in French as *figue de barbarie* (Barbary fig) – Barbary being the old name for the North African coast. However, it is not an indigenous plant, since cacti are native only to the deserts of south-western, North and Central America. It was introduced to North Africa soon after the discovery of the Americas and has flourished ever since.

Another example is the ubiquitous mint tea of Morocco. This would appear to be an ancient tradition, yet in reality it dates from as recently as 1854, when British merchants needed an alternative outlet for their wares that could not be sold in eastern Europe and Turkey owing to the Crimean War. They sold the tea cheaply in Tangiers and Essaouira (the modern name for Mogador), and the Moroccans adapted it to their own tastes, substituting milk with fresh mint leaves.

Right: Beans, grains and pulses are sold in bulk in African markets. Note the variety of measuring equipment.

EUROPEAN COLONISTS

Southern Africa, with its variety of terrains, including more temperate climates suitable for wheat cultivation, is the most heavily influenced by the foods of the former colonists. There is strong Portuguese influence in Angola and Mozambique, British influence in Zimbabwe, and British and Dutch influence in South Africa.

French influence

Not surprisingly, with its strong food culture, French food has influenced all the former French possessions, and the baguette is as universal in North and Saharan Africa as is the local flat bread. Pâté from chicken livers is another French introduction, and coffee is ground and drunk the French way. French cooking styles have had a beneficial effect on local dishes, including such delights as yam soufflé (*soufflé d'ignames*), eaten in

Below: A woman slices fish in Kayar, Senegal, where fresh fish is plentiful.

Madagascar. Vegetables from French seeds such as carrots, French (green) beans and cabbage are added to stews of local foods in Senegal, where French influence is strongest and ties to France are among the closest in Africa.

Portuguese influence

The Portuguese influence on African cooking has been extremely important, with the contribution of two basic Portuguese foods: capsicums (chilli and bell peppers) and dried cod. The peppers, originally brought from South America, have permeated the whole of Africa, with Tunisia, Saharan and West Africa being particularly fond of peppery stews spiced with large amounts of small chilli peppers. Dried fish, usually dried cod or hake, is imported into Africa in large amounts. This is an important protein element in countries in which protein is scarce and expensive. The cod is soaked in several changes of water for 24 hours, then

steamed or boiled with *foufou* and vegetables, including the ubiquitous chilli sauce (piri-piri) or chilli peppers.

Asian influence

The foods of the Republic of South Africa are also heavily influenced by the large population who came from the Indian subcontinent and very much by the "Cape Malays". These were settlers from south-east Asia, the former Malaya, Singapore and Indonesia, who arrived in the 19th century at the same time as the Indians, and who had an important influence on the national diet.

Merchants from the Indian subcontinent, whose highly spiced curries are very much in tune with the African palate, have also influenced the local cuisine. The fragrant curries of Kenya, Tanzania and South Africa, especially in cities with a large population from the subcontinent, such as Mombasa and Durban, are typical of Indian and Pakistani influence.

AFRICAN FEASTS AND FESTIVALS

Each African country enjoys its own regional dishes, sometimes influenced by their religious beliefs but more often by the ingredients that are available to them. In many parts of Africa meat is an important part of celebratory eating as it is not eaten on a daily basis.

NORTH AFRICA

Islamic traditions dictate social customs and entertaining in the countries of North Africa. For example, during the month of Ramadan, when eating and drinking are forbidden during daylight hours, each country has its own traditional food on which to break the fast in the evening. In most of North Africa, Harira, a soup made with chickpeas or lentils, will be served; however, in Egypt it will be a dish made from lentils and rice known as Mejedra.

In the Horn of Africa, Muslims celebrate both Eids (the two Muslim festivals of ul-Fitr and ul-Adha) with *sheer korma*, made with vermicelli and various nuts, including pistachio nuts, almonds and charoli nuts. The charoli nut is similar to a hazelnut and is found all over Asia and in Muslim Africa.

Whole sheep and goats are roasted for religious festivals, such as Eid, and in parts of the Maghreb, camels are also eaten. Stuffed camel stomach is a delicacy that may be served at a Moroccan feast for celebrating a special occasion such as a wedding. Naturally, there will be a dish of couscous, often a couscous royale, a massive dish where the grain is piled high in a huge metal dish, garnished with vegetables and sprinkled with rosebuds. This will be accompanied by a spicy sauce made from the stock in which the vegetables were stewed, laced with spices – ground cumin, saffron, ginger, chilli pepper and cardamom.

Choua, a dish of stewed lamb, may also be served, and the elegant pigeon pie known as Bastilla as well as other pies made with phyllo (or filo) dough. The meal will be rounded off by apricots, almonds, dates, figs and sweetmeats, such as baklava or halva. No alcohol is consumed as it is forbidden to Muslims.

SUB-SAHARAN AFRICA

In the countries of sub-Saharan Africa, which are predominantly non-Muslim, the feasts that are reserved for religious festivals and weddings may last for days. In Kenya, no wedding feast is complete without *ugali*, a kind of maize porridge, which can also be made from millet or cassava flour. *Ugali* is often accompanied by green bananas, wrapped in banana leaves and cooked on open fires. Another accompaniment to *ugali* and green bananas is *chiswa*, white ants or termites boiled and then fried. Perhaps more to European taste are the *simsim balls*: made from toasted, ground sesame seeds, which are also served with the maize porridge.

In Nigeria, a festive meal will include Chicken Suya, grilled chicken with a fragrantly spicy coating. The classic Nigerian dish, Jollof Rice, is always on offer, as well as fried plantains and bean porridge, a spicy stew of field

Above: The feast of Eid ul-Fitr marks the end of Ramadan. Here in the market of Habta in Sharqiya, Egypt, men are buying food for the celebration.

beans. Beans also feature in the snack food called Ackroes: fried bean cakes served to visitors, which are also available from street stalls all over Nigeria. Puff-puff – little puffs of fried dough – and meat pies are also served as appetizers at parties, although they can also be bought in the street. In the Cameroon, a wedding feast will certainly feature a dish called Folon, a stew of chicken and prawns (shrimp) flavoured with coconut water and folon leaf, a bitter leaf native to the Cameroon.

In sub-Saharan tropical Africa, palm wine and beer are the favourite drinks for celebrations: Star Beer in Ghana, Tusker Beer in Kenya. Local breweries can be found throughout the region, but many still prefer to drink Guinness.

SOUTHERN AFRICA

Celebrations in South Africa usually centre on the barbecue, known as a *braai* (pronounced "bry"). These barbecues originated as spit roasts in the late 17th century at celebrations held by the Dutch governor of what is now Cape Province. Later, the voortrekkers, the Dutch settlers, had to cook their meat in this way due to lack of other facilities. Cooks in different regions use different ingredients for the braai. In the Karoo, the central desert, mutton, lamb and eland are popular. In Natal, on the east coast, barracuda and yellowtail fish are wrapped in banana leaves and served with typical Zulu accompaniments such as mealies (corn on the cob), cornmeal breads and fritters. The South African lager, Castle, is popular as well as their wide range of sherries and wines.

On the island of Madagascar the wedding feast will be of fresh seafood and rice, as well as manioc flour (gari or tapioca) to accompany the Romazava: a meat and vegetable stew spiced with ginger. *Ranovola*, a watery rice drink, is

Below: Men of the Masai tribe roast a white bull for the festival of Olingsher, when boys of the village come of age.

enjoyed at celebrations, and in the north of the island there is *trembo* (fermented coconut juice).

Sweetmeats of various kinds are always served at weddings. Particular favourites include coconut and honey sticks in Mali, and *kashata na nazi* (coconut candy) in Uganda. These are the same sweets that are served for any other kind of entertaining. Pastries are

Above: In rural Africa weddings involve the entire community. Here Sudanese men participate in a wedding dance.

always popular: the Arab *sambusak* metamorphosed into the Indian samosa, and both are served throughout Africa. These small triangular pastries may be filled with either sweet or savoury mixtures before being fried.

AFRICAN INGREDIENTS

In the arid regions of Africa all foods are scarce and precious, and are carefully prepared. The favourite grains, rice and millet, maize and acha, are pounded and dried then made into a liquid porridge or couscous-like cooked grain. Dried beans, dried *meloukhia* and dried okra are sometimes the only vegetables available, supplemented during the rainy season with squashes, fresh beans and green leafy vegetables. Fermented foods – pickles, rancid clarified butter and yogurt – are important items of the diet, as are dried fish, sardines and prawns (shrimp), in areas away from lakes and the sea. Fish is an important item of diet where it is available, mainly Nile perch and tilapia.

GRAINS

A wide range of grains is eaten: various types of millet, including finger millet (*eleusine*), sorghum and teff (in the Horn of Africa). The main staples are rice in Egypt and couscous, cracked grain, usually durum wheat, in the Maghreb (Algeria, Morocco and Tunisia). Couscous is sometimes made from barley, especially among the

Kabyles of Algeria. Sesame (*simsim* or *benné*) is an African plant that is rich in oil and, like peanuts, the oil can be extracted and used for cooking.

Above: Fishermen work in the water and on traditional boats for tuna and pomfret in the Indian Ocean, off the coast of Mombasa, Kenya.

PROTEIN

Because meat is expensive and scarce in most parts of the African continent, certainly among the poor and the tribal peoples, vegetable protein is extremely important. This is provided by the native peanut and other varieties of nuts, and various types of beans and peas throughout the continent. Almonds grow in North Africa and are often added to savoury dishes, such as couscous. Kola nuts are popular because they act as a stimulant. They grow in the tropical rainforests of West Africa and are chewed fresh, or dried and ground to a powder for making into a drink. One type can be found as far south as Angola. The seeds may be white or pink, but purple is preferred. The nut is often eaten as a digestive before a

Left: Grains play a central part in the African diet, and are still farmed using traditional methods.

meal, as it is claimed that its slightly bitter flavour makes food subsequently eaten taste sweet. It is customary for a bride and groom to exchange kola nuts at a Nigerian wedding. Similar to the kola nut is the misnamed Java olive, which grows throughout Africa.

Black-eyed beans (peas) and cowpeas are typical ingredients in Africa's classic stews, which mainly consist of vegetables and dried beans, occasionally supplemented with a little fish, and even more occasionally with meat or poultry.

Fish are valuable adjuncts to the diet and both saltwater and freshwater fish are eaten all over the continent, as are prawns, shrimps and mussels.

Meat comes in the form of lamb and goat, camel (mainly for festive occasions), and game such as gazelle and cane-rat (also known as *agouti*). All over Central Africa wild game, known as "bush meat" is eaten: including kudu and eland, and, in parts of West Africa, even monkey.

In areas where dairy cattle are bred, such as among the Dinka peoples, whose territory extends across southern Sudan, Uganda and northern Kenya, the animals are a sign of wealth. As such they are far too valuable to be slaughtered. The dairy herds are, however, regularly bled from the neck and the nutrition-rich blood is mixed with *chisaka* – African spinach or amaranth – and stewed. This mixture is eaten with *ugali* (maize meal).

Below: Spices are used extensively in Africa, and are often made into mixes.

FRUIT AND VEGETABLES

A wide variety of fruits are grown in the region, many of them unknown and unavailable outside Africa. Vegetables are an important ingredient in Africa, especially leaves and greens, but also staples such as yams and plantains.

DAIRY PRODUCTS

Fermented milks of all kinds are widespread. Many peoples simply milk their flocks and pour the liquid into a gourd that is left in a tree for four or five

Below: Many varieties of nuts are cultivated in Africa, but also grow wild.

Above: Cloves are spread out to dry in the sun on the island of Zanzibar.

days until the milk has fermented. Fermented milk, yogurt and butter are often given to children.

SPICES

Spices are a favourite and essential ingredient in African cuisine. Some are produced and sold locally, but most of them are grown in East Africa on the island of Zanzibar.

Below: Giant snails and prawns, popular in Ghana, are used to flavour stews.

PRESERVED FOOD AND OILS

Refrigeration is still rare in much of Africa, but advancements in modern food preservation techniques, especially canning, have been a boon to tropical Africa. Pickled, dried and preserved food is an African tradition that continues to be as important today as it was in the past. Alongside the mounds of colourful fruits and vegetables, the open-air markets feature huge cans of condensed milk and butter or ghee (clarified butter or vegetable fat), as well as corned beef and lamb to supplement the meagre diet in the arid lands. Oils extracted from nuts and seeds are also used in different parts of the continent.

PRESERVES

Dried and puréed tomatoes are popular ingredients. It is not unusual to see women sieving and drying tomatoes on large mats in villages. Garden eggs – aubergines (eggplants) – are also dried for use when they are out of season.

Below: Various types of vegetables are pickled throughout Africa, peppers and turnips are particular favourites.

DRIED FISH

In areas of Africa away from lakes or the sea, dried fish is an important part of the diet. Many kinds are dried, including sardines, prawns and shrimps, which are used mainly in stews. However, salt cod, eaten widely in sub-Saharan Africa, is imported.

CANNED AND BOTTLED FOODS

As well as canned tomatoes and tomato purée (paste), which are imported, there are many locally produced canned and bottled foods that are used in African cooking.

Pickles

Vegetables pickled in brine are eaten throughout the continent. In North Africa, pickles (*torshi*) are made from aubergines, turnips, (bell) peppers, onions, and cucumbers, usually coloured pink with beetroot juice.

Smen

Used throughout Africa, smen is clarified butter used for cooking. It is also preserved and laid down in the

Above: Dried shrimps and anchovies are both used in African stews.

same way that Europeans lay down vintage wines. Sometimes it is preserved for many years, stored in jars and kept in cellars.

Spiced ghee and shea butter

In Ethiopia, *niter kebbeh*, or spiced ghee, is used for cooking. This is made by adding onion, garlic, ginger, turmeric, cardamom, cinnamon, clove and nutmeg to unsalted (sweet) butter.

Shea butter is a solid fat prepared from the seeds of a tree found in Ghana and Nigeria. The oval fruits contain a thin pulp and a large, oval, shiny brown seed. The pulp is allowed to rot away through exposure to the sun and the kernels are then roasted and pounded to make butter. The Hausa people of northern Nigeria prefer not to roast the nut before its butter is extracted. The fat then extracted is less odorous and more to European taste. Shea butter is also boiled in water and exported to Europe where it is added to margarine. It is also used in cosmetics.

Dairy fats

Fermented milk and butter are very important in the African diet. Buttermilks and mixtures that are a kind of intermediate stage between yogurt and clarified butter are used in cooking and added to all types of foods to enrich them. Buttermilks are often given to babies that are being weaned and to young children. In Senegal, a thick buttermilk mixture known as *nebam*

sirne is highly prized as a cooking medium. It is mostly home-made but small factories have begun producing it commercially. *Nebam sirne* may also be used fresh or, like smen, be kept for years to mature.

Coconut

Coconut milk is available in cans and can be stored indefinitely. A favourite cooking medium, creamed coconut is used for many types of fried snacks sold as street food in tropical Africa.

OILS

As well as smen, there are several varieties of oils that are used for cooking throughout Africa.

Palm oil

Also known as palm kernel oil, palm oil is reddish in colour, due to its high vitamin A content. It is made from the kernel of a palm tree native to West and Central Africa, from Benin to the Congo Valley, and is a valuable export. The nut produced by this palm is the dendé nut. This is a rare example of an African food travelling to South America. It was probably taken to Brazil by Portuguese slave traders; at any event it is now popular there, especially in the province of Salvador, whose inhabitants are largely of African origin. The fibrous pulp of the dendé nut is very oily, and the stone (pit), which is the size of a

Above: A selection of oils used in African cooking: in front is coconut oil, palm oil on the left and olive oil on the right. The oils at the back are corn oil on the right and the lighter groundnut oil on the left.

Below: Shea butter, bottom, and coconut cream, top, are highly nutritious fats used African cooking.

walnut, has a white, oily kernel. In the 19th century, Europeans realized the potential of palm oil for making margarine, as it solidifies much more quickly than other vegetable oils. Palm oil is exported from tropical Africa.

Nut oils

Other oils used in African cooking include peanut, sesame seed and corn, which are all crushed and their oil extracted. Sesame oil has a strong flavour and fragrance and is used in dishes that can withstand it.

Bush butter is derived from a tropical tree that is known as the African pear, native pear, *safu* or *eben*. The purplish plum-sized fruit grows in tropical Africa and is added to stews and curries. It has a high protein content.

Other oils

Cotton oil is an important oil for cooking in the dry areas of the continent that produce the finest cotton. The biggest African producers, and also exporters, of cotton oil are Egypt and the Sudan.

Sunflower oil is a lighter oil, which is used in Kenyan and Nigerian cooking, especially for frying.

Olive oil is also used, especially in North African countries, although less extensively than elsewhere in the Mediterranean region.

GRAINS, BEANS AND SEEDS

Africa has a variety of staple foods, filling starches for a continent where famine is not uncommon. To complement the grains are many different beans and lentils, another important form of protein.

GRAINS

In the more temperate climates of North Africa – Egypt, Algeria, Morocco and Tunisia – where the climate allows for as many as three wheat or barley harvests a year, the staple grains are coarsely ground to make couscous. Millet and sorghum are grains that are used for animal feed outside Africa, but here they are important ingredients in the human diet.

Wheat

The wheat used to make couscous is a hard wheat: durum wheat. Wheat is also made into bread: the flat breads of North Africa or the thick, porous *injera* of Ethiopia, which is used as much as an eating implement as a food, for mopping up the rich, thick sauces of Ethiopian stews known as *wat*. .

Rice

Another staple eaten in all parts of the continent is rice, which is grown in Egypt, along the Nile, and other river valleys in Africa. The so-called Carolina rice was introduced into the United States from Africa by the slave ships, which carried it to feed their human cargo. This rice variety is still cultivated and eaten throughout tropical Africa and in Egypt.

Right: Green (top) and grey, or Puy lentils (bottom) grow wild around the Mediterranean and are a valuable vegetable protein.

Cornmeal

The other universal grain is cornmeal or maize, originally imported from the Americas in the 16th century. Maize is dried and served as cornmeal for use as a thickener for stews, such as *kenkey* and *banku*, both eaten in the Congo with spicy vegetable stews.

Millet

Also known as *acha*, *giro*, hungry rice and *fonio*, millet has been long used in western Europe as birdseed but is gaining popularity as a healthy, wholegrain food. It is another popular staple in Africa. The nutty, slightly bitter flavour combines well with stews. It is native to Africa, looks a little like maize,

Left: Two African varieties of grain, Carolina rice (top) and millet or acha (bottom), and sesame seeds (middle).

and grows about 4m/13ft tall, like corn on the cob. It is a fast-growing crop that needs little water, so it flourishes in the dryer parts of the continent. It stores well without deteriorating, which is another reason for its popularity in the Horn of Africa, where drought and famine are not unknown.

Millet is mixed with other food in some countries: in Nigeria, for example, it is mixed with baobab grain or the dry pulp of the baobab fruit.

Sorghum

Also known as *dawa* or guinea corn, sorghum is related to millet and is native to the drier uplands, and has been cultivated in Ethiopia for thousands of years. It is also especially popular in West Africa. Two varieties, black African and white pearl, are popular for grinding into a porridge, but because the grain contains no gluten it cannot be made into bread. Certain cultivars have sap in their thick stems that can be turned into syrup. It will not crystallize into grains because it does not have enough sucrose. Sorghum syrup is dark brown and sticky and tastes a little like molasses, but it has a milder flavour.

Teff

The teff seed is an important grain in Ethiopia. It is the smallest grain seed: 150 grains being equal in size to one grain of wheat. It is low in gluten and high in protein and carbohydrates, a good source of calcium and iron, and high in fibre, and consequently has become the latest fashionable wholegrain in the United States and western Europe and is now available from health food stores.

Cassava

Known by various names, including *gari,* cassava flour may be made in the home, but it is also produced commercially. It is cooked with water and eaten as a filling staple.

Above: Cassava flour (top) and cornmeal are staples of sub-Saharan Africa and come from South America. They are eaten with stews.

DRIED BEANS

All types of bean are valuable additions to the diet in Africa. The field bean, the forerunner of the broad (fava) bean, is a staple in the Egyptian diet, as are lentils – both the puy and the green.

Chickpeas

Native to North Africa, chickpeas feature in stews and all savoury dishes, although they are also coated with icing sugar and eaten as candies in the

Below: The peanut (groundnut) is native to Africa, and is a legume or pulse, like a pea or bean. The pods develop underground, hence its name.

winter. Chickpeas are almost always found dried, but they are in season in May, and fresh green chickpeas are a delicious snack eaten in Egypt and throughout North Africa. The Indian influence is apparent where chickpeas are split after drying and made into channa dhal. This is then fried as chickpea fritters. These fritters are popular all along the coasts of West and East Africa and in South Africa.

Field beans

In Egypt, the day usually begins with a bowl of ful medames – field beans stewed in water, with olive oil, lemon juice, cumin, onion and garlic, sometimes with the addition of a quartered hard-boiled egg.

Pigeon peas

Like all varieties of peas, pigeon peas are native to Africa. They may be eaten fresh or dried and, if very young, boiled in the pod. When dried, they are added to soups and stews.

Peanuts

Known for their high protein and fat content, peanuts are native to Africa and an important ingredient where animal protein is scarce. Mainly known as groundnuts, peanuts are cooked in stews. They also yield valuable groundnut oil. Groundnut stew is the national dish of Ghana, a stew that includes meat and aubergines as well as roasted peanuts. It is served with rice and small side dishes of raw onion rings, banana slices sprinkled with cayenne pepper, chutney, grated coconut and more toasted peanuts. Peanuts are grown in large plantations and are exported, dried, roasted or as oil, to Europe. Peanut flour is mixed with other flours to enrich the diet.

SEEDS

Benné, or sesame seed, is another highly nutritious native African plant. The seeds may be toasted and ground,

Above: Field beans are used to make ful medames, which is considered the national dish of Egypt. These beans are also known as horse-beans.

and served with honey or sugar as cakes, or sprinkled on savoury rice or other starches to enrich the main meal. The oil from the seed is also used for adding flavour to cooking.

The oil-yielding niger seed is from the same family as the sunflower but is native to East Africa, and is cultivated in Ethiopia. Niger seeds are eaten fried, in pickles or in cakes. The oil the seeds yield has a nutty flavour, and is sometimes used as a substitute for ghee or smen.

Below: Blackeyed peas or beans (top) and pigeon peas (bottom) take the place of the field bean in sub-Saharan Africa as a source of protein.

SPICES AND HERBS

One feature that is typical of African food throughout the continent is the love of spices and, in particular, hot peppery sauces. Fresh herbs are less widely used, and are mainly lemongrass, mint, basil and rocket.

SPICES

Many of the spices used in African cooking were imported by the Arab traders, but are now grown locally or come from East Africa, the Sudan, Ethiopia and, especially, Zanzibar. The climate and growing conditions in the picturesque island of Zanzibar, with its strongly Arab-influenced culture and lifestyle, are similar to those of the original Spice Islands: the Dutch East Indies. In the early 18th century, the Arabs brought spices to Zanzibar, now also known as Spice Island, for cultivation, and the island still supplies much of Africa with these essential cooking ingredients.

The island is still the prime source of the world's supply of cloves, and, unsurprisingly, cloves are used extensively in the cookery of the region. Other spices grown in Zanzibar are pepper, cardamom, ginger and nutmeg. These spices are important in the local cuisine, which is heavily influenced by the large population from the Indian subcontinent. Curry powder, also known as *mchusi*, has become a much-used ingredient in the African kitchen, thanks

to the Asian influence from traders and settlers. As well as these cultivated and exported spices, there are also spices that are native to Africa, and which still grow wild throughout the region. These include dried baobab leaves and fruits, and grains of selim (also known as African nutmeg). Okra, when dried, is also used as a spice. Potash, from the Bitter Lakes, is used as a substitute for salt and as a raising agent. Egusi seeds, the seeds of certain varieties of watermelon, are used to flavour soups, and are beneficial to the diet owing to their oil content.

Saffron

The classic spice of North Africa is saffron. Once grown even as far north as the United Kingdom (as in Saffron Walden), the saffron crocus is now mainly grown in Morocco, and is exported around the world. In North

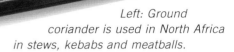

Left: Ground coriander is used in North Africa in stews, kebabs and meatballs.

African cooking it is an important ingredient in a variety of stews and is used to flavour and colour rice with its subtle fragrance and bright yellow hue. Another spice that is used in African cooking for its rich yellow colour, as well as its flavour, is turmeric.

Cloves

Cloves were originally imported from the Spice Islands by the Arabs, who traded extensively along the East Coast of Africa. They are grown throughout northern and eastern Africa and used lavishly in cooking. In Zanzibar, cloves are chewed to sweeten the breath.

Ginger

Ginger, like cloves, is used in many African dishes, and is a particularly favourite spice for flavouring stews.

Nutmeg

The fruit seed is about the size of an apricot. It has a lacy covering known as mace, which tastes similar to the nut and is also used as a spice. Nutmeg is used in sweet and savoury dishes.

Below: Ginger root can be used fresh, but more often is dried and used in its powdered form.

Below: Saffron, the most prized and rare of all spices, has a subtle taste and imparts a golden colour to food.

Below: Turmeric, also known as the poor man's saffron, has a stronger flavour and is extensively used in Indian-influenced dishes.

Above: Scotch bonnets are colourful African varieties of chilli pepper that are also grown in the West Indies.

Chillies

The hot peppers used to make the dipping sauces and pastes are almost certainly an import from South America from the days of the early traders in the 17th century, although this applies to many foods in Africa, because the climates of both continents are similar. In fact, there was a local pepper that was used in quantity before chillies became available. It is known as *melegueta* pepper or, more poetically, as grains of paradise. The plant is a tall reed that has elongated red and orange

Below: Chilli powder is a preservative, which kills bacteria on fresh food, an added benefit in hot countries where food quickly becomes bad.

fruits. These fruits contain as many as 100 seeds, which are the "grains of paradise" themselves. Melegueta pepper became popular in Europe soon after West Africa was discovered by explorers, and was shipped in large quantities, but its popularity declined and it is now hard to find outside its native area.

SPICE MIXES

These include the ras el hanout of Algeria and Morocco, the harissa of Tunisia, the berbere of Ethiopia and the pilpil of Angola and Mozambique. In North Africa, Tunisian dishes are the most fiery, with Algeria and Morocco tending to favour more subtle flavours. Tunisian harissa, usually the famous Le Phare du Cap Bon variety, can now be found in food stores all over the world in its distinctive yellow "toothpaste" tube.

Berbere

This is an Ethiopian blend of spices added to many local dishes, from baked fish to chicken stews.

8 white cardamoms
10 dried red chillies
5ml/1 tsp cumin seeds
5ml/1 tsp coriander seeds
5ml/1 tsp fenugreek seeds
8 cloves
5ml/1 tsp allspice berries
10ml/2 tsp black peppercorns
5ml/1 tsp ajowan seeds
5ml/1 tsp ground ginger
2.5ml/½ tsp ground nutmeg
15ml/1 tbsp salt

Heat a heavy frying pan. Bruise the cardamom pods and add to the pan with the chillies, cumin, coriander, fenugreek, cloves, allspice, peppercorns and ajowan seeds. Toast the spices until they give off a rich aroma. Remove the seeds from the cardamoms and discard the husks. Grind all the spices to a fine powder. Mix in the ginger, nutmeg and salt. You can use the mix at once or store it in a jar.

All three countries of the Maghreb make extensive use of a mixture called ras el hanout (meaning "head of the shop") consisting of as many as twenty spices dominated by cumin and hot red pepper, although the mixture varies depending on where it is made. In Ethiopia, bitter spices and herbs, such as fenugreek and ajwan, are included in spice mixtures and added to stews.

In Egypt, the classic spice mixture is a dried one known as duqqa (which derives from an Arabic word meaning "pounded"). The ingredients in duqqa, and their proportions, vary from one family to another but generally include sesame and coriander seeds, dried crushed mint, salt and pepper. It may also include chickpea flour and crushed millet. It is usually sprinkled on bread dipped in olive oil.

HERBS

Fresh herbs are used less than spices in African cooking. Lemongrass is used in Kenya, strongly influenced as it is by its Asian population. Lemongrass can be dried, whole or shaved, powdered or distilled into a fragrant oil. It has a fragrant citrus flavour and aroma.

Basil was known in ancient Egypt and is still used in many Egyptian dishes. Mint is an essential ingredient for mint tea in the Maghreb, and flat leaf parsley is used lavishly in many soup and salad recipes as an ingredient in its own right.

Below: Lemon grass is used extensively in the cooking of Kenya. It can be shaved and dried, as here.

FRESH VEGETABLES

African cooking has always placed great reliance on locally grown fresh vegetables, and in spite of imported or canned foods, this is still the case.

Green leafy vegetables

A winter luxury in the arid lands, green leafy vegetables are available only when the summer sun does not shrivel the leaves. *Meloukhia* is a green, spinach-like vegetable with a slightly slimy consistency that is used to make soup and added to stews in Egypt and Saharan Africa. Spinach is used in stews and fritters. Bitterleaf is another variety of green vegetable available in East and West Africa. The leaves of bean plants and pumpkins are eaten as green vegetables. Cassava leaves are also eaten.

Amaranth, also known as African spinach, is another popular green vegetable. Marrow greens and cowpea leaves are enjoyed, as are sweet potato tops, which, unlike the tops of ordinary potato, are not poisonous.

Above: Turnips and their tops are an essential ingredient in the stew that accompanies couscous in North Africa.

The leaves of other root vegetables are also added to soups and stews in Africa. No part of the plant is wasted; turnip tops and mustard greens (still eaten in the southern states of the USA by people of African origin) and the green leaves of okra (a type of hibiscus) are all added to soups and stews. The tough, fibrous leaves of the banana and plantain are used as disposable plates and to package foods, such as gari (cassava or tapioca flour) for steaming and boiling. In West Africa, a favourite way to use green

vegetables is in palaver sauce. Whatever green leaves are available are used to make this sauce, although it should always contain bitterleaf. A little meat, including offal (variety meats), and shellfish are added, as well as watermelon, or egusi, seeds. The mixture is then sprinkled with palm oil. The dish is known as *plassas* in Sierra Leone and *ban flo* in Ghana.

The green leaves of the manioc plant are the main ingredients in *kpwem*, a soup from southern Cameroon. The leaves should be as young and tender as possible. They are stewed with ground peanuts and a little palm oil.

Squashes

Pumpkins, squashes and gourds all flourish in the heat, and many varieties of these are eaten, even the liffa, the gourd from which loofahs are made. Squashes and pumpkins are particularly popular, finding their way into most stews. Gourds are not only eaten but are also used as containers (calabashes), utensils (cut in half and used as ladles) and as drinking vessels.

Aubergines

In Kenya, aubergine is known as eggplant or *brinjal*, the latter being the

Below: From top to bottom, cocoyam, cassava yam, guinea yam (left) and soft yam (right).

Above: Pumpkin is an important food all over Africa, mainly as an ingredient for stew. In Libya, it is pickled and mashed and eaten with couscous.

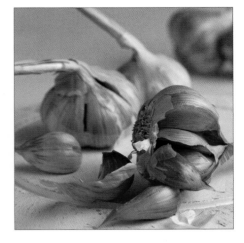

Above: Okra is valued for the gelatinous texture it gives to stews and soups. It is also known as gumbo.

Above: Plantains are members of the banana family. They are eaten green or ripe, baked or boiled or fried.

Above: Garlic, the pungent Mediterranean plant, is used extensively as a flavouring all over Africa.

Right: Ackee is usually sold in cans.

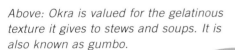

Indian name. Garden eggs are a white or greenish-yellow variety of aubergine, which are eaten mainly in West Africa. A favourite Nigerian dish is chicken gumbo, for which chicken is stewed with garden eggs.

Okra

Gumbo is also another name for okra, the vegetable that is perhaps most closely associated with Africa. In North Africa, okra is deep-fried in oil, which eliminates any trace of sliminess. However, the slimy texture is valued elsewhere in Africa, for the bulk it gives to stews.

Peppers

Chilli peppers and sweet (bell) peppers, known as bell chillies, are eaten all over the continent. They vary in size and shape from tiny red birdseye chillies and so-called cherry peppers to larger, elongated, milder green (bell) peppers.

Yams

The cocoyam and Guinea soff yam are varieties of yam that are probably indigenous to West Africa. The Guinea

soff yam is known locally as *allato*; it may be white or yellow. Yellow yams should not be confused with the sweet potato, which is often known as yellow yam in the United States.

Ackee

Now associated principally with Jamaica, the ackee was originally introduced there from West Africa in the

Below: Bell peppers or capsicums, originally from central and South America, are popular in North African cooking.

18th century. The fruit is fluffy and yellow like scrambled egg, but the centre is poisonous, so ackee is always sold canned outside its native habitat.

Plantains

A member of the banana family, plantains are inedible raw, and are cooked extensively in Africa in many different ways.

OTHER VEGETABLES

Colocassia is a root eaten since antiquity, when it was Europe's equivalent of the potato. Colocassia is still eaten widely in Africa, as are eddoes, a taproot related to colocassia. Tomatoes, potatoes and carrots were introduced by the Europeans. The onion, garlic, and other members of the allium family are grown throughout northern Africa.

FRESH FRUIT

Africa is famous for its fruits, although many of the native fruits are rarely seen outside the continent, baobab fruits being one example. The baobab is a huge tree that grows all over tropical Africa, from Senegal to Zimbabwe, and can live to be 3,000 years old. It is very strange looking in that the branches look more like roots, as if it were growing upside down. The fruit, which grows up to 30cm/1ft long, contains tartaric acid and vitamin C, and can either be sucked or soaked in water to make a refreshing drink. The fruits are also dried and roasted then ground up to make a coffee-like drink or used as a flavouring and spice.

Other wild fruits, which grow in Kenya, are *muratina*, *burarakambi*, *chufutu* and *busemwa*. Many fruits that are considered to be indigenous are, in fact, not native to the continent, such as orange, tangerine, coconut, banana, mango and papaya.

Surinam cherry

The acerola, or Surinam cherry, originally from the Caribbean, has become very popular in the Horn of Africa. It cannot be eaten fresh as it is too acidic, but makes wonderful jams, jellies and preserves.

Citrus fruit

Imported via India, most citrus fruits probably originally came from China. They have taken to the African climate and are available throughout the year, which makes them widely used. They have largely been spread not by human plantations but by birds, especially

Right: Tangerines are cultivated in Algeria, and are harvested between the months of November and April.

parrots, and grow wild in the forests of Kenya and Zimbabwe. Of course, they are carefully cultivated in North Africa, and Algeria has produced its own varieties, such as the clementine and the tangerine, which are an important Christmas export.

Banana

It is surprising to think that bananas, which are an African staple, are not native to the continent, but originally came from India. In addition to the fruit itself, which is eaten ripe, as a fruit, or unripe, as a vegetable, the leaves make wrappers for food, and disposable plates. Green

bananas are certain unripe varieties that are used as a vegetable. They are boiled, with or without their skins.

African horned melon

Also known by the name of kiwano, this extraordinary fruit is bright orange and covered with small bumps or protrusions. The flesh is green and it has small crunchy pips similar to passion fruit.

Dates and figs

Luscious dates and figs are native to coastal regions of North Africa. They are dried and exported southwards to Saharan and sub-Saharan Africa. Dates are important in the practice of Islam, as the prophet Mohammed

Right: Prickly pears come from the opuntia cactus. The flesh inside is sweet, though full of seeds.

Below: Jackfruit or jakfruit are large fruits with nutritious seeds that must be boiled before being eaten.

Below: Dates are ideal food for hot regions as in their dried form they keep for months.

Below: The kiwano, or African horned melon, is spectacular with its bright orange skin, thick spines, green flesh and black seeds.

advocated breaking the Ramadan fast by eating dates and drinking water. Figs are mainly found in North Africa, and are used in desserts, as well as eaten fresh and dried.

Locust bean

Also known as carob, this bean grows in the drier parts of North Africa on a large, handsome tree. The long brown beans have a sweet pulp, which is enjoyed by children and also fed to domestic animals. The beans are also fermented and then cooked with the *meloukhia* leaf, especially in Saharan Africa, where the resulting dish is known as *crain crain*.

Below right: Physalis is grown in, and exported widely from, Cape Province, hence its other name of Cape gooseberry.

Physalis

Also known as a Cape gooseberry, the physalis looks like an orange cherry, encased in a papery calyx, and is rich in vitamin C. It is often used for decoration because of its attractive appearance. Despite the profusion in which it grows around the Cape of Good Hope in South Africa, it is really a native fruit of Peru.

Jackfruit

Another fruit originally from the Indian continent is the jackfruit, the largest of the tree-born fruits. It can weigh as much as 41kg/90lb. The fruit growing on the tree is a strange sight because it grows directly out of the trunk on a short stem. Inside the fruit, the thick, warty flesh is yellow, very sweet, and firm rather than fibrous. The large seeds, known as jacknuts, are also edible but are eaten boiled.

The jackfruit has an unpleasant smell, but this does not permeate the flesh. The flesh must be eaten as soon as it is ripe because the fruit will continue to ripen after the flesh is cut.

Below: Pineapples are have become an important import from the Ivory Coast.

Cactus fruit

Also known as prickly pear, this small greenish-orange fruit is from the opuntia cactus, the cactus fruit is native to the Americas, and possibly China, and was introduced into the Middle East and North Africa by merchant traders in the 16th century.

Pineapple

Just as Kenya is famous for its exports of vegetables, most of which were originally from the Americas, so the Ivory Coast and Malawi are exporters of another South American fruit, the

Right: Watermelon is an African native fruit that has spread all over the world.

pineapple. Miniature pineapples, grown more for their beauty than their usefulness, are also exported.

Grapes

Vines are indigenous to North Africa and there has always been a flourishing wine trade there. Algeria, Morocco and Tunisia also all produce table grapes, and raisins, for export.

Watermelon

The watermelon has been grown in Africa for centuries and is depicted on Egyptian wall paintings, although earlier varieties were small and probably bitter. They are now universally sweet and very large and are grown throughout Africa. The two main varieties of watermelon are round with a dark-green skin and deep-red flesh, or elongated with a pale green skin or a skin striped with darker green. Watermelons were taken to the Americas via the slave trade.

FISH AND SHELLFISH

Fresh fish and shellfish are found all along the coasts. Fishing methods in Africa (except for South Africa) remain traditional: fish are speared or caught in nets by fishermen in boats working as a team, and lake fish are often netted by a single fisherman. Fish forms a vital part of the African diet, even inland, although the problem of keeping fish fresh is a serious one where refrigeration is still a luxury.

Thébouidienne is a classic fish stew from Senegal, in which any white fish is stewed slowly in a casserole with cabbage, sweet potato, bell chillies, pimentos and chilli peppers. The stew is served on a bed of rice. In the Ivory Coast, the fish is casseroled similarly, but the flavourings are pumpkin, marrow and fresh coconut, strips of which are laid over the fish. To this is added rice, fried onions and seasoning, it is then simmered in coconut water until tender.

FRESH FISH

The following fish are to be found in the rivers or seas of the African continent, but they can all be substituted with similar-sized white fish that may be more easily available.

Below: The brightly coloured parrot fish is popular in West Africa.

Nile perch and tilapia

Both these freshwater fish are eaten in Egypt and the Sudan, with the Nile perch the most frequently consumed. They are usually fried in oil.

Jobfish

A member of the snapper family, the jobfish lives in the waters of the Indian Ocean and is sold along the coast in Kenya, Tanzania and Mozambique. It is an attractive orange or lavender colour.

Above: Red mullet is an important catch in the Mediterranean and is used for a variety of North African dishes.

Red mullet

Among the finest of all sea fish, the flesh of red mullet is lean and firm, and its flavour is robust and distinctive. Because of this, red mullet is a favourite in North African countries, where it is used in a wide variety of dishes. It is caught in the Mediterranean, so does not feature in the more southern areas of Africa.

Parrotfish

The parrotfish is a colourful fish that lives on coral reefs, and is popular in the fish stews of West Africa. In Liberia, it is often cooked with coconut cream and served with *foufou* (mashed cassava or yam). The fish are sautéed in butter or ghee, seasoned with salt and pepper and fried. They are then stewed in coconut milk in a covered pan. The cover is then removed and the sauce reduced until it is creamy.

Other species

In West and South Africa, it is the fish of the southern Atlantic that are caught, including grey mullet and albacore, swordfish and marlin as well as species

Cape Kedgeree

Although originally a curry, Cape kedgeree from South Africa is no longer a spicy dish, owing to the influence of the British and Dutch. Fish that has been precooked – usually red mullet or snoek – is mixed with cooked rice (there should be twice as much fish as rice) and chopped egg whites. It is then seasoned with salt and pepper and simmered in evaporated milk or single cream. The yolks of hardboiled eggs are then pushed through a sieve and used to garnish the dish before it is served.

of shark and snoek. In East Africa, the best ocean catch is considered to be shark, known as *papa*, which is mainly cut into strips, dried and sent inland. The snoek is an oily fish and as such is particularly delicious dried or smoked. Other varieties used are yellowtail, steenbrass and Hottentot fish.

DRIED FISH

A highly prized ingredient in Africa, many different types of small fish are dried and used extensively for flavouring foods. Particular favourites are dried anchovies, which are sold in great piles

Below: Oysters are often eaten as an appetizer in the restaurants of Kenya.

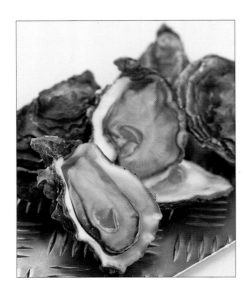

Above: Salt cod before soaking.

in all African markets, and used in meat dishes as well as fish-based recipes such as the stews of Senegal and Mali, Uganda, Kenya and Tanzania. In the western Cape province, fatty fish including mullet and herring are strung up in bunches to dry in the sun, to make a dried fish called *hardums*.

Fish calulu is an Angolan fish stew, which is made from a mixture of dried and fresh fish. The dried fish are softened in hot water then stewed with the fresh fish, seasoned with garlic, salt, vinegar and lemon. Alternate layers of the dried and fresh fish are then placed in a large pan with sliced onion, tomatoes, spinach or sweet potato leaves and sliced okra. This is then simmered in palm oil until cooked. The rich stew is usually served with a manioc flour porridge known as *funge*.

Salt fish

Also known as stockfish, salted cod is an important ingredient in cooking throughout sub-Saharan Africa. The fish is imported from countries bordering the North Atlantic, such as Portugal. It is rock hard when purchased, and needs soaking for at least 24 hours in several changes of water before it is ready for cooking.

In Tanzania, the cod is made into a stew called *dagaa*, which is made with tomatoes, onions, chilli and coconut milk.

SHELLFISH

Seafood is a particular favourite of South Africans, where freshly caught lobsters and scallops are widely available. Throughout the rest of Africa shrimps or prawns are dried, and used as flavourings.

Oysters

The oysters of the East African coast are said to be the most delicious in the world. They are regularly served as an appetizer in Kenyan restaurants, European-style with rose-marie sauce and wedges of lemon.

Prawns and shrimps

In Egypt, fresh prawns (shrimp) are a favourite appetizer. In Nigeria they are made into pancakes, using a batter made from ground white haricot beans, tomatoes, onions, cooked prawns and eggs. The pancakes are deep fried, and are often available as street food.

The Indian influence in South Africa is obvious from the fish curries that are often made with prawns. The curries are served with rice and a variety of raitas, such as onion rings, bananas, sliced cucumbers, chutney and shredded coconut. A similar curry is made in East Africa, with small shrimps.

Below: Fresh prawns (shrimp) are a popular ingredient, and when dried they are used extensively throughout Africa.

MEAT AND POULTRY

Red meat is a luxury, especially in central Africa, but poultry, such as the guinea fowl, a bird native to Africa and probably domesticated here as long as five thousand years ago, is an important source of meat. In Africa, meat and fish are often cooked together in the same dish, especially in the former Portuguese colonies of Angola and Mozambique, in a dish known as *futu*, which should have twice as much meat as fish.

RED MEAT

The most popular red meats in the Maghreb (Algeria, Morocco and Tunisia) and Saharan Africa, where the animals are raised for milk and meat as well as for their skins or fleece, are that of sheep and goats. The meat is ground, or it might be cut into small pieces or ground with spices and spit-roasted. It may also be added to stews. Only kid is roasted, as older goat is too tough and so it is usually boiled or stewed. Curried goat is a popular dish in Nigeria, and *nyama choma* is very popular in Kenya. This dish consists of goat kebabs served with cooked green banana mash.

Below: Goat is popular in Kenya and Nigeria; it is a tough meat that needs long, slow cooking.

Above: Beef is a luxury food throughout Africa, except in South Africa, where cattle are bred for meat.

Above: Lamb, in chunks or minced, is the favourite meat of North African cuisine.

In those parts of Kenya and the Sudan where herders count their wealth in cattle, the animals are too valuable to be eaten, so beef is not commonly eaten in East Africa. The Masai, for

Below: Buffalo is one of the game meats that is hunted and eaten in Africa.

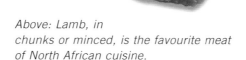

example, would never eat cattle. However, it is extremely popular in South Africa, where it is used is many different ways, including curries and barbecues. In the Cameroon it is stewed in a fragrant curry with coconut and pineapple. Hump-backed cattle, or zebu, of the type found in India, are also bred in Africa, although more for their milk than meat.

Although pork is forbidden by Islamic law, and not eaten in Muslim countries, it is popular among non-Muslims in West and South Africa in the form of stews and barbecued spare ribs.

GAME

The cane-rat or grasscutter (known as *agouti* in French-speaking Africa) is a rodent that may be as much as 60cm/24in long, not including the tail. It is widely eaten in sub-Saharan Africa. The bush-pig is related to the wart-hog and is eaten in tropical Africa. It has a gamey flavour, tasting more like wild boar. In Central Africa, even monkey and bat are eaten. Gazelle, kudu, eland and other game animals are also eaten in the savannah and in the Sahel, where they roam. Ostrich has lately gained in popularity, as the red meat is lean and flavoursome. The Cape buffalo is hunted and eaten in Africa. The meat from most of these game animals can be airdried and smoked to make biltong.

INSECTS

In Africa, insects are widely eaten, and are a good source of free protein, including grubs, white ants, termites and especially locusts. Plagues of locusts were once common, and eating them was a good way of getting animal protein and helping to protect the crops at the same time, as they were caught before they could damage the crops. Those who have eaten locusts describe them as delicious: crunchy on the outside and creamy within.

Other insects that are eaten include crickets, grasshoppers and flying ants. Even worms and caterpillars are sold as

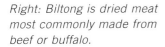

Right: Biltong is dried meat most commonly made from beef or buffalo.

fried snacks, in towns and cities as well as in more isolated rural areas.

BILTONG

In Southern Africa, and South Africa in particular, beef and other lean meats can be seasoned and dried to make biltong. Game is often preserved this way, including animals such as eland, zebra and ostrich, A long piece of muscle is trimmed into an oval shape and then rubbed with salt, pepper, coriander and fennel. The meat is soaked in vinegar and left to marinate for a few days. It is then hung up in the open air to dry in the wind. When dried out, it is smoked.

If made from game, the biltong is so hard that it can be grated. In South Africa it is often eaten this way as a snack, on top of buttered bread.

CHICKEN

Eggs and chicken are important items in the diet of the those who live in the cities, and those who can afford it put chicken in their stews. Chicken eaten in town or cities in Africa may be the plump, domesticated fowl or even broiler fowl, but in the villages all over Africa chickens roam freely and are consequently lean and tough.

Broiling chicken is known in French West Africa as *poulet bicyclette* (bicycle chicken). No one quite knows why this term is used, perhaps because they are as lean as if they had kept fit by riding a bicycle, but more probably because they are kept for laying and eaten only if they are unfortunate enough to be "road kill". These chickens need long, slow cooking in stews such as Ashanti Chicken from Ghana, where the chicken is slow-cooked with yams, tomatoes and mint leaves, and Yassa Chicken, a traditional recipe from the Camance region of Senegal. Here the chicken is first fried in peanut oil, then slowly stewed in

water with spices, including mustard and chilli peppers, lemon juice, vinegar, cabbage and carrots for at least six hours. It is served with *foufou*, cooked and mashed green banana, or rice. Rabbit and guinea fowl can be treated in the same way.

In Angola, chicken is often barbecued (grilled), such as peri-peri chicken, where the bird is first marinated in paprika, hot chilli powder, lemon juice, cloves and ginger.

In North Africa, rich omelettes similar to those eaten in Iran are popular. Chicken irio, a Kikuyu dish from Kenya, is made from eggs, puréed beans, maize and potatoes or cassava, and served with curried chicken.

PIGEON

In the Maghreb and Egypt, pigeon is also an important food item. Pigeons are raised in special towers and their meat is used in roast pigeon with pine nuts and honey or in Bastilla, the famous Moroccan pie.

GUINEA FOWL

There are four species of guinea fowl, all of which are native to Africa, and their ranges extend from the north to south of the Sahara. Guinea fowl were probably domesticated by the ancient Egyptians, but they are expensive and eaten mainly on feast days.

Above: Pigeon is a great delicacy in Egypt and Morocco, where the birds are bred for the table.

Below: Guinea fowl is a domesticated bird that is native to Africa. The flesh is well flavoured and gamey.

BREADS AND BEVERAGES

Africa is the home of bread, for it is here that the ancient Egyptians first mixed flour with water and left it in the sun. The natural yeasts in the air did the rest. Similarly, most beverages are based on fermentation, including the so-called palm wines of Central Africa.

BREADS AND PASTRIES

In Africa breads are generally flat breads made from wheat. The Ethiopians have two main forms of bread. One is *hambasha*, a firm dough kneaded like a European bread and flavoured with black onion seed or nigella, ground cumin and ground coriander. *Injera* is made with a loose dough, usually made with teff, an indigenous grain grown in the Ethiopian highlands. *Injera* is eaten as a bread, but it is also laid flat on the table and used like the trencher of the Middle Ages – a kind of edible plate on which stew is poured, allowing the bread to soak up the juices as the meal progresses. Diners also use the bread to scoop up meat and vegetable stews. For this purpose, it is cut into long strips.

Phyllo or brik dough is a thin pastry dough, almost identical to filo pastry or strudel dough. One of its uses is to make a pastry from Tunisia that has a filling of egg, vegetables and tuna.

BEVERAGES

Two of the most universally drunk beverages in the world, coffee and beer, were given to the world by Africa.

Above: Phyllo, *the pastry dough that is the trademark of Moroccan cooking.*

Coffee and tea

The coffee shrub grows wild in Ethiopia, and the beans are harvested both from the wild plant and from cultivated varieties. The Ethiopians prefer to dry the beans just until they are still green, then roast and grind them as needed. The coffee drunk all over North and Saharan Africa is prepared in the same way as in the Middle East: ground to a powder, then added to water and boiled over an open fire. Sometimes cardamom or cinnamon is added. In southern Africa coffee is made by percolating rather than boiling, and in South Africa it is drunk with milk.

Below: Flat bread, baked on stones or on the floor of the oven, is probably similar to ancient Egyptian bread.

Tea, both black and green varieties is grown in East and West Africa. In the Maghreb it is taken with a form of spearmint, which is particularly aromatic, rather than milk. Copious amounts of tea are drunk throughout Africa, with meals and on its own. Like coffee, it is the drink of hospitality. Red tea, or Rooibos is a herbal tea that is a favourite drink in South Africa.

Milk

Fresh milk is a luxury in hot climates without refrigeration, but goat's milk and fermented milks (yogurt and kefir-type drinks) are drunk in tropical Africa. Camel milk is also drunk in the Sahara.

Beer

Originally, beer was invented by the ancient Egyptians, who baked cakes of barley then let them ferment in water to produce a rich yeast, beer being an accidental by-product of the process. Thus, beer was developed before people discovered what an improvement yeast made when added to the baked paste of water and flour that came to be eaten as bread. Africans now consume much less beer than people on other continents: about 9 litres/16 pints per capita per year, compared to 21 litres/37 pints as a world average.

Tusker beer is the national drink of Kenya: a light, refreshing beer that

Below: Castle lager, South Africa's most popular beer. All non-Muslim African countries brew their own brands.

Above: Tusker beer, Kenya's own brand, is exported widely, and very much appreciated by Kenyan expatriates.

Above: Coconut water, left, is often drunk in a cocktail. Van der Hum, right, is South Africa's coffee liqueur.

should be drunk ice cold. There are also breweries producing alcohol-free beers, including ABC in Egypt. In South Africa, apart from the popular lagers and ales, such as Castle lager, beer is also brewed illegally and sold at unlicensed bars, known by the Irish name of "shebeens".

Spirits and liqueurs

In Madagascar, rum and fermented coconut water are popular drinks, especially in the north of the island. Africans also brew and distil alcohol from millet. Palm wine is made in tropical Africa. Van der Hum is a liqueur made from brandy and rum steeped in orange peel, orange blossoms, cloves, nutmeg, cinnamon and cardamom. It was originally made by the Dutch settlers, and was named after the Dutch admiral who liked it.

WINES OF AFRICA

Grape-growing began in Algeria in ancient times, and wines were even exported to Rome. Viticulture was revived in 1830, with the arrival of French colonists. In the 1870s, vineyards in France were ravaged by the insect pest phylloxera, and many wine-makers moved to Algeria, where they planted the best French vine

stocks. The vineyards are concentrated in three regions: Oran, Constantine and Algiers. The grape varieties grown are mainly Cinsault, Carignan and Grenache, but in some regions Cabernet, Syrah and Merlot are also used. Although the wines of Algeria have suffered from a poor reputation in the past, they are improving. Red wines account for 65 per cent of production, owing to the southern climate, although there are some good whites, especially Coteaux du Zaccar and Médéa. In Oran, Oued-Imbert wines are red, white and rosé. The red wines are generally heavy, coarse and dark, with a high alcohol content and low acidity. They are mainly exported to France, to be blended with wines of the Midi to increase their low alcohol content and add colour and body.

Tunisian vines grow mainly around Cap Bon. Many are dessert wines of the muscat variety, and some of the reds are mixed with rectified spirit to produce a drink called mistelle. The rosé wines are considered among the best in North Africa. Moroccan wines

Right: Fairview Pinotage, on the right, is made with a grape created in South Africa. Danie de Wet Chardonnay is a white wine that has won great praise.

come mainly from the region around Meknès, although vines are grown in Rabat, Casablanca, Fez, Oujda and Marrakech. There are white and red grapes, one variety of which, the Rafsai white grape of the Rif mountain region, is now being vinified. North-eastern Morocco produces rosé wines of comparable quality to Algeria's.

The wines of South Africa have a well established reputation. The first vine cuttings were brought there in 1654, probably from the Rhineland. Wine was made in the Cape by the Dutch colonists for the first time in 1659. The French Huguenots, who first arrived in 1688 and settled in the Franschek Valley, extended the vineyards and improved the quality of the vines. Today, the two vine-growing areas are the Coastal Belt and the Little Karoo. Harvesting is between February and April, before autumn. Many of the vineyards grow in beautiful countryside, presided over by period Dutch plantation houses, some still owned by the original families.

SOUPS,
APPETIZERS
AND SNACKS

In some African countries, the first course is seen as a main component of the meal, rather than simply a morsel to tempt the appetite. This chapter introduces some of the soups, appetizers and snacks you may encounter, and whether you sample them on your travels or recreate them in your home, you'll discover a world of new and fascinating flavours, from exquisite soups to sweet and spicy nibbles.

MOROCCAN PUMPKIN SOUP

MODERN MOROCCAN STREET STALLS AND MARKETS ARE PILED HIGH WITH COLOURFUL SEASONAL PRODUCE. THE PUMPKIN SEASON IS PARTICULARLY DELIGHTFUL, WITH THE HUGE ORANGE VEGETABLES DISPLAYED ON TABLES AND WOODEN CARTS. THE SELLERS PATIENTLY PEEL AND SLICE THE PUMPKINS READY FOR MAKING THIS SIMPLE AND TASTY WINTER SOUP, WITH ITS HINT OF SUGAR AND SPICE.

SERVES FOUR

INGREDIENTS
    about 1.1kg/2lb 7oz pumpkin
    750ml/1¼ pints/3 cups
      chicken stock
    750ml/1¼ pints/3 cups milk
    10–15ml/2–3 tsp sugar
    75g/3oz/½ cup cooked white rice
    salt and ground black pepper
    5ml/1 tsp ground cinnamon,
      to garnish

COOK'S TIPS
Use butternut squash in place of
pumpkin. Use cooked brown rice in
place of white rice, if preferred.

1 Remove any seeds or strands of fibre
from the pumpkin, cut off the peel and
chop the flesh. Put the prepared
pumpkin in a pan and add the stock,
milk, sugar and seasoning.

2 Bring to the boil, then reduce the
heat and simmer for about 20 minutes,
until the pumpkin is tender. Drain the
pumpkin, reserving the liquid, and
purée it in a blender or food processor,
then return it to the pan.

3 Bring the soup back to the boil again,
throw in the rice and simmer for a few
minutes, until the grains are reheated.
Check the seasoning, pour into bowls
and dust with cinnamon. Serve piping
hot, with chunks of fresh, crusty bread.

Energy 148Kcal/627kJ; Protein 8.8g; Carbohydrate 20.7g, of which sugars 13.5g; Fat 4g, of which saturates 2.3g; Cholesterol 11mg; Calcium 308mg; Fibre 2.8g; Sodium 81mg.

CHORBA WITH RAS EL HANOUT AND NOODLES

THIS FULL-FLAVOURED CHORBA IS THE DAILY SOUP IN MANY MOROCCAN HOUSEHOLDS. THE RAS EL HANOUT GIVES IT A LOVELY, WARMING KICK. YOU CAN PURÉE THE SOUP, IF YOU PREFER, BUT HERE IT IS LEFT AS IT IS, FINISHED OFF WITH A SWIRL OF YOGURT AND FINELY CHOPPED CORIANDER. GARLIC LOVERS MAY LIKE TO ADD A CRUSHED GARLIC CLOVE AND A LITTLE SALT TO THE YOGURT.

SERVES FOUR

INGREDIENTS
  45–60ml/3–4 tbsp olive oil
  3–4 whole cloves
  2 onions, chopped
  1 butternut squash
  4 celery sticks, chopped
  2 carrots, chopped
  8 large, ripe tomatoes
  5–10ml/1–2 tsp sugar
  15ml/1 tbsp tomato purée (paste)
  5–10ml/1–2 tsp ras el hanout
  2.5ml/½ tsp ground turmeric
  a big bunch of fresh coriander
    (cilantro), chopped
  1.75 litres/3 pints/7½ cups
    vegetable stock
  a handful of dried egg noodles or
    capellini, broken into pieces
  salt and ground black pepper
  natural (plain) yogurt, to garnish

1 Peel, seed and cut the squash into small chunks. Skin, and roughly chop the tomatoes. In a deep, heavy pan, heat the oil and add the cloves, onions, squash, celery and carrots. Fry until they begin to colour, then stir in the chopped tomatoes and sugar. Cook until the liquid reduces and the tomatoes begin to pulp.

2 Stir in the tomato purée, ras el hanout, turmeric and chopped coriander. Pour in the stock and bring the liquid to the boil. Reduce the heat and simmer, uncovered, for 30–40 minutes until the vegetables are very tender and the liquid has reduced a little.

3 To make a puréed soup, let the liquid cool slightly before processing in a blender or food processor, then pour back into the pan and add the pasta.

4 Alternatively, to make a chunky soup, simply add the pasta to the unblended soup and cook for a further 8–10 minutes, or until the pasta is soft.

5 Season the soup to taste and ladle it into bowls. Spoon a swirl of yogurt into each one, garnish with coriander sprigs and serve with a freshly baked Moroccan loaf.

Energy 265Kcal/1108kJ; Protein 6.9g; Carbohydrate 37.8g, of which sugars 20.2g; Fat 10.2g, of which saturates 1.7g; Cholesterol 0mg; Calcium 158mg; Fibre 8.1g; Sodium 64mg.

LAMB, BEAN AND PUMPKIN SOUP

ASIDE FROM THE GREEN BANANAS, WHICH ARE VERY MUCH AN AFRICAN TOUCH, THIS SOUP COULD HAVE COME FROM ANY OF THE LANDS OF THE MIDDLE EAST. PUMPKIN, CARROT AND TURMERIC GIVE IT A RICH COLOUR AND THE SPICES PROVIDE A WARMTH DESIGNED TO BANISH WINTER CHILLS.

SERVES FOUR

INGREDIENTS
  115g/4oz black-eyed beans (peas),
    soaked for 1–2 hours, or overnight
  675g/1½lb neck of lamb, cut into
    medium-size chunks
  5ml/1 tsp chopped fresh thyme, or
    2.5ml/½ tsp dried
  2 bay leaves
  1.2 litres/2 pints/5 cups stock
    or water
  1 onion, sliced
  225g/8oz pumpkin, diced
  2 black cardamom pods
  7.5ml/1½ tsp ground turmeric
  15ml/1 tbsp chopped fresh coriander
    (cilantro)
  2.5ml/½ tsp caraway seeds
  1 fresh green chilli, seeded
    and chopped
  2 green bananas
  1 carrot
  salt and ground black pepper

1 Drain the beans, place in a pan and cover with cold water. Bring to the boil and boil rapidly for 10 minutes, then reduce the heat and simmer, covered, for 40–50 minutes until tender, adding more water if necessary. Remove from the heat and set aside to cool.

2 Meanwhile, put the lamb in a large pan, add the thyme, bay leaves and stock or water and bring to the boil. Cover and simmer over a medium heat for 1 hour, until tender.

3 Add the onion, pumpkin, cardamoms, turmeric, coriander, caraway seeds, chilli and seasoning and stir. Bring back to a simmer and then cook, uncovered, for 15 minutes, until the pumpkin is tender, stirring occasionally.

4 When the beans are cool, spoon into a blender or food processor with their liquid and process to a smooth purée.

5 Cut the bananas into medium slices and the carrot into thin slices. Stir into the soup with the bean purée. Cook for 10–12 minutes, until the vegetables are tender. Adjust the seasoning and serve.

Energy 442Kcal/1855kJ; Protein 40.8g; Carbohydrate 27.2g, of which sugars 13.1g; Fat 19.7g, of which saturates 9g; Cholesterol 128mg; Calcium 74mg; Fibre 6.4g; Sodium 155mg.

GHANAIAN FISH AND OKRA SOUP

OKRA GROWS WELL IN MANY PARTS OF WEST AFRICA AND THE SUDAN, AND SOUPS LIKE THIS ONE WERE THE INSPIRATION FOR GUMBO, WHICH SLAVES INTRODUCED TO THE CARIBBEAN AND NORTH AMERICA. OKRA THICKENS THE SOUP AND GIVES IT A UNIQUE TEXTURE AND FLAVOUR.

SERVES FOUR

INGREDIENTS

2 green bananas
50g/2oz/¼ cup butter or margarine
1 onion, finely chopped
2 tomatoes, skinned and
  finely chopped
115g/4oz okra, trimmed
225g/8oz smoked haddock
  or cod fillet, cut into
  bitesize pieces
900ml/1½ pints/3¾ cups
  fish stock
1 fresh red or green chilli, seeded
  and chopped
salt and ground black pepper
chopped fresh parsley,
  to garnish

1 Slit the skins of the bananas and place in a large pan. Cover with water, bring to the boil and cook over a medium heat for 25 minutes. Drain.

2 Melt the butter or margarine in a large pan and sauté the onion for about 5 minutes. Stir in the tomatoes and okra and sauté for a further 10 minutes.

3 Add the fish, fish stock, chilli and seasoning. Bring to the boil, then reduce the heat and simmer for about 20 minutes, until the fish is cooked through and flakes easily.

4 Peel the cooked bananas and cut into slices. Stir into the soup, heat through for a few minutes and then ladle into soup bowls. Sprinkle with chopped parsley and serve.

Energy 295Kcal/1233kJ; Protein 20g; Carbohydrate 24.6g, of which sugars 21.2g; Fat 13.8g, of which saturates 7.5g; Cholesterol 47mg; Calcium 477mg; Fibre 12.7g; Sodium 532mg.

PLANTAIN AND CORN SOUP

CAMEROON IS THE HOME OF THIS COLOURFUL AND UNUSUAL SOUP. IT IS IMPORTANT TO USE RIPE PLANTAINS, WHICH COOK DOWN AND BECOME BEAUTIFULLY TENDER. NUTMEG ADDS THE FINAL TOUCH.

SERVES FOUR

INGREDIENTS

25g/1oz/2 tbsp butter or margarine
1 onion, finely chopped
1 garlic clove, crushed
275g/10oz yellow plantains, peeled
  and sliced
1 large tomato, peeled and chopped
175g/6oz/1 cup corn
5ml/1 tsp dried tarragon, crushed
900ml/1½ pints/3¾ cups vegetable
  or chicken stock
1 fresh green chilli, seeded
  and chopped
pinch of freshly grated nutmeg
salt and ground black pepper

1 Melt the butter or margarine in a pan over a medium heat, add the onion and garlic and sauté for a few minutes until the onion is soft.

2 Add the plantains, tomato and corn and cook for 5 minutes.

3 Add the tarragon, vegetable or chicken stock, chilli and salt and pepper and simmer for 10 minutes or until the plantain is tender. Stir in the nutmeg and serve immediately.

GROUNDNUT SOUP

GROUNDNUTS — OR PEANUTS — ARE VERY WIDELY USED IN SAUCES IN AFRICAN COOKING. GROUNDNUT PASTE IS AVAILABLE FROM MANY HEALTH FOOD SHOPS AND IS WORTH SEEKING OUT AS IT MAKES A WONDERFULLY RICH AND CREAMY SOUP.

SERVES FOUR

INGREDIENTS

45ml/3 tbsp pure groundnut paste
  or peanut butter
1.5 litres/2½ pints/6¼ cups stock
30ml/2 tbsp tomato purée (paste)
1 onion, chopped
2 slices fresh root ginger, peeled and
  finely chopped
1.5ml/¼ tsp dried thyme
1 bay leaf
salt and chilli powder
225g/8oz white yam, diced
10 small okras, trimmed (optional)

1 Place the groundnut paste or peanut butter in a bowl, add 300ml/½ pint/1¼ cups of the stock and the tomato purée and blend together to make a smooth paste.

2 Spoon the nut mixture into a pan and add the onion, chopped ginger, thyme, bay leaf, salt, chilli powder and the remaining stock. Heat gently until the liquid is simmering.

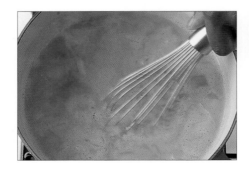

3 Cook for 1 hour, stirring from time to time to prevent the nut mixture sticking.

4 Add the white yam and cook for a further 10 minutes. Add the okra, if using, and simmer until tender. Serve.

COOK'S TIP
Use peanut butter in place of groundnut paste, but only use the smooth variety for this recipe.

TOP Energy 185Kcal/775kJ; Protein 5.8g; Carbohydrate 22.6g, of which sugars 5.2g; Fat 8.3g, of which saturates 1.9g; Cholesterol 0mg; Calcium 66mg; Fibre 3.3g; Sodium 75mg.
BOTTOM Energy 198Kcal/837kJ; Protein 2.7g; Carbohydrate 35.6g, of which sugars 11g; Fat 6g, of which saturates 3.4g; Cholesterol 13mg; Calcium 20mg; Fibre 2.3g; Sodium 162mg.

CHICKEN, TOMATO AND CHRISTOPHENE SOUP

CHRISTOPHENE IS A PALE GREEN GOURD. IN SOUTHERN AFRICA IS IS CALLED CHO-CHO, WHILE ELSEWHERE IT IS CALLED CHOKO, CHAYOTE OR VEGETABLE PEAR. THE FLESH HAS A DELICATE FLAVOUR.

SERVES FOUR

INGREDIENTS
  225g/8oz skinless, boneless
    chicken breasts
  1 garlic clove, crushed
  pinch of freshly grated nutmeg
  25g/1oz/2 tbsp butter or margarine
  ½ onion, finely chopped
  15ml/1 tbsp tomato purée (paste)
  400g/14oz can tomatoes, puréed
  1.2 litres/2 pints/5 cups
    chicken stock
  1 fresh red or green chilli, seeded
    and chopped
  5ml/1 tsp dried oregano
  2.5ml/½ tsp dried thyme
  1 christophene, about 350g/12oz
    total weight, peeled and diced
  50g/2oz smoked haddock fillet,
    skinned and diced
  salt and ground black pepper
  chopped fresh chives, to garnish

1 Dice the chicken, place in a bowl and season with salt, pepper, garlic and nutmeg. Mix well to flavour the chicken and then set aside for about 30 minutes.

COOK'S TIP
Christophene is a vegetable of the squash family native to central America. The flesh is crisp and light green in colour, and the flavour is delicate and very mild. It may be used in a similar way to courgettes (zucchini) in cooking.

2 Melt the butter or margarine in a large pan, add the chicken and sauté over a medium heat for 5–6 minutes. Stir in the onion and sauté gently for a further 5 minutes, until the onion is slightly softened.

3 Add the tomato purée, puréed tomatoes, stock, chilli, dried herbs and christophene. Bring to the boil, cover and simmer gently for 35 minutes, until the christophene is tender.

4 Add the smoked fish, simmer for a further 5 minutes, until the fish is cooked through, adjust the seasoning and pour into warmed soup bowls. Garnish with a sprinkling of chopped chives and serve.

Energy 133Kcal/558kJ; Protein 16.7g; Carbohydrate 3.2g, of which sugars 2.4g; Fat 6g, of which saturates 3.5g; Cholesterol 57mg; Calcium 36mg; Fibre 1.1g; Sodium 167mg.

CAMEROON VEGETABLE SOUP

COCONUT CROPS UP IN MANY POPULAR CAMEROONIAN DISHES, INCLUDING THEIR FAMOUS BEEF AND PINEAPPLE CURRY. HERE IT IS TEAMED WITH SWEET POTATO AND SPICES TO MAKE A TASTY SOUP.

SERVES FOUR

INGREDIENTS
   30ml/2 tbsp butter or margarine
   ½ red onion, finely chopped
   175g/6oz each turnip, sweet potato
      and pumpkin, peeled and
      roughly chopped
   5ml/1 tsp dried marjoram
   2.5ml/½ tsp ground ginger
   1.5ml/¼ tsp ground cinnamon
   15ml/1 tbsp chopped spring onion
      (scallion)
   1 litre/1¾ pints/4 cups
      well-flavoured vegetable stock
   30ml/2 tbsp flaked (sliced) almonds
   1 fresh red or green chilli, seeded
      and chopped
   5ml/1 tsp sugar
   25g/1oz creamed coconut or
      60ml/4 tbsp coconut cream
   salt and ground black pepper
   chopped fresh coriander (cilantro),
      to garnish

COOK'S TIP
Take care when preparing fresh chillies. Avoid touching your eyes and wash your hands thoroughly afterwards (or wear disposable gloves).

1 Melt the butter or margarine in a large non-stick pan. Fry the onion for 4–5 minutes. Add the chopped vegetables and fry for 3–4 minutes.

2 Add the marjoram, ginger, cinnamon, spring onion, salt and pepper. Sauté over a low heat for about 10 minutes, stirring frequently.

3 Add the vegetable stock, flaked almonds, chilli and sugar and stir well to mix, then cover and simmer gently for 10–15 minutes, until the vegetables are just tender.

4 Grate the creamed coconut into the soup, or add the coconut cream, and stir to mix. Spoon the soup into warmed bowls and serve, sprinkled with chopped coriander.

Energy 168Kcal/701kJ; Protein 2.3g; Carbohydrate 13.2g, of which sugars 5.5g; Fat 12.2g, of which saturates 7.9g; Cholesterol 16mg; Calcium 50mg; Fibre 2.4g; Sodium 66mg.

ROASTED RED PEPPERS WITH FETA, CAPERS AND PRESERVED LEMONS

RED PEPPERS, PARTICULARLY THE LONG, SLIM, HORN-SHAPED VARIETY, FEATURE WIDELY IN THE COOKING OF NORTH AFRICA. ROASTING THEM REALLY BRINGS OUT THEIR SMOKY FLAVOUR AND THEY TASTE WONDERFUL WITH CRUMBLED WHITE CHEESE. FETA IS SUGGESTED HERE, BUT VILLAGERS WOULD JUST USE WHATEVER WAS AVAILABLE LOCALLY, WHETHER FROM GOAT'S, EWE'S OR COW'S MILK. THIS DISH MAKES A GREAT FIRST COURSE AND ALSO TASTES GOOD WITH KEBABS.

SERVES FOUR

INGREDIENTS

4 fleshy red (bell) peppers
200g/7oz feta cheese, crumbled
30–45ml/2–3 tbsp olive oil or
  argan oil
30ml/2 tbsp capers, drained
peel of 1 preserved lemon, cut into
  small pieces
salt

1 Preheat the grill (broiler) on the hottest setting. Roast the red peppers under the grill, turning frequently, until they soften and their skins begin to blacken. (Alternatively, spear the peppers, one at a time, on long metal skewers and turn them over a gas flame, or roast them in a very hot oven.)

2 Place the peppers in a plastic bag, seal and leave them to stand for 15 minutes. Peel the peppers, remove and discard the stalks and seeds and then slice the flesh and arrange on a plate.

3 Add the crumbled feta and pour over the olive or argan oil. Scatter the capers and preserved lemon over the top and sprinkle with a little salt, if required (this depends on whether the feta is salty or not). Serve with chunks of bread to mop up the delicious, oil-rich juices.

Energy 255Kcal/1058kJ; Protein 9.6g; Carbohydrate 12g, of which sugars 11.4g; Fat 19.1g, of which saturates 8.2g; Cholesterol 35mg; Calcium 194mg; Fibre 2.8g; Sodium 727mg.

ARTICHOKE HEARTS WITH GINGER, HONEY AND LEMONS

WHEN GLOBE ARTICHOKES ARE IN SEASON, THEY GRACE EVERY MOROCCAN TABLE AS A FIRST COURSE OR SALAD. THE HEARTS ARE OFTEN POACHED IN SALTED WATER UNTIL TENDER, THEN CHOPPED AND TOSSED IN OLIVE OIL WITH GARLIC, HERBS AND PRESERVED LEMON. FOR A MORE EXCITING APPETIZER, THE ARTICHOKES ARE COOKED IN A GLORIOUS SPICED HONEY DRESSING. PRESERVED LEMONS, WHICH ARE AVAILABLE IN LARGE JARS AT EVERY NORTH AFRICAN MARKET, ADD A PIQUANT NOTE.

SERVES FOUR

INGREDIENTS
30–45ml/2–3 tbsp olive oil
2 garlic cloves, crushed
scant 5ml/1 tsp ground ginger
pinch of saffron threads
juice of ½ lemon
15–30ml/1–2 tbsp clear honey
peel of 1 preserved lemon,
  thinly sliced
8 fresh globe artichoke hearts,
  quartered
150ml/¼ pint/⅔ cup water
salt

1 Heat the olive oil in a small, heavy pan and stir in the garlic. Before the garlic begins to colour, stir in the ginger, saffron, lemon juice, honey and preserved lemon.

2 Add the artichokes to the pan and toss them in the spices and honey. Pour in the water, add a little salt and heat until simmering.

3 Cover the pan and simmer for 10–15 minutes, until the artichokes are tender, turning them occasionally.

4 If the liquid has not reduced, take the lid off the pan and boil for about 2 minutes until reduced to a coating consistency. Serve at room temperature.

COOK'S TIP
To prepare globe artichokes, remove the outer leaves and cut off the stems. Carefully separate the remaining leaves and use a teaspoon to scoop out the choke with all the hairy bits. Trim the hearts and immerse them in water mixed with a squeeze of lemon juice to prevent them from turning black. You can use frozen hearts for this recipe.

Energy 115Kcal/478kJ; Protein 0.8g; Carbohydrate 15.6g, of which sugars 15g; Fat 5.9g, of which saturates 0.9g; Cholesterol 0mg; Calcium 32mg; Fibre 3g; Sodium 32mg.

SPINACH AND CHICKPEA PANCAKES

PANCAKES ARE POPULAR IN THOSE AFRICAN STATES THAT HAVE AT SOME TIME BEEN OCCUPIED BY THE FRENCH. THESE HAVE A SPINACH AND CHICKPEA FILLING; HIGH ON FLAVOUR, LOW ON SPICE.

SERVES FOUR TO SIX

INGREDIENTS
15ml/1 tbsp olive oil
1 large onion, chopped
250g/9oz fresh spinach
400g/14oz can chickpeas, drained
2 courgettes (zucchini), grated
30ml/2 tbsp chopped fresh
   coriander (cilantro)
2 eggs, beaten
salt and ground black pepper
fresh coriander (cilantro) leaves,
   to garnish
For the pancake batter
150g/5oz/1¼ cups plain
   (all-purpose) flour
1 egg
about 350ml/12fl oz/1½ cups milk
15ml/1 tbsp sunflower or olive oil
butter or oil, for greasing
For the sauce
25g/1oz/2 tbsp butter
30ml/2 tbsp plain (all-purpose) flour
about 300ml/½ pint/1¼ cups milk

1 First make the pancakes. Whisk together the flour, a little salt, the egg, milk and 75ml/5 tbsp water to make a fairly thin batter. Stir in the oil.

2 Heat a large griddle, grease lightly and fry the pancakes on one side only, to make eight large pancakes. Set aside while preparing the filling.

3 Heat the oil in a frying pan and fry the onion for 4–5 minutes until soft. Wash the spinach, place in a pan and cook until wilted, shaking the pan occasionally. Chop the spinach roughly.

4 Skin the chickpeas: place them in a bowl of cold water and rub them until the skins float to the surface. Mash the skinned chickpeas roughly with a fork. Add the fried onion, grated courgettes, spinach and chopped coriander. Stir in the beaten eggs, season and mix well.

5 Place the pancakes, cooked side up, on a work surface and place spoonfuls of filling down the centre. Fold one half of the pancake over the filling and roll it up. Place in a large, buttered ovenproof dish and preheat the oven to 180°C/350°F/Gas 4.

6 Melt the butter for the sauce in a small pan, stir in the flour, and then gradually add the milk. Heat gently, stirring continuously, until the sauce is thickened and smooth. Simmer gently for 2–3 minutes, stirring. Season with salt and pepper and pour over the pancakes.

7 Bake in the oven for about 15 minutes, until golden and then serve garnished with coriander leaves.

Energy 560Kcal/2351kJ; Protein 26.2g; Carbohydrate 68.2g, of which sugars 14.8g; Fat 22.1g, of which saturates 7.5g; Cholesterol 166mg; Calcium 473mg; Fibre 8.6g; Sodium 472mg.

SCHLADA

THIS DISH FROM MOROCCO IS A GOOD EXAMPLE OF HOW RECIPES MIGRATE. IT BEGAN AS AN ANCIENT ARAB DISH CALLED GAZPACHO, WHICH MEANS "SOAKED BREAD". THE MOORS TOOK THE RECIPE TO SPAIN. AT THAT STAGE, THE INGREDIENTS WERE SIMPLY GARLIC, BREAD, OLIVE OIL AND LEMON JUICE. THE SPANISH LATER ADDED TOMATOES AND PEPPERS, AND THE DISH RETURNED TO NORTH AFRICA, WHERE IT BECAME KNOWN AS SCHLADA, AND ACQUIRED SPICES AND PICKLED LEMON.

SERVES FOUR

INGREDIENTS
    3 green (bell) peppers, quartered
    4 large tomatoes
    2 garlic cloves, finely chopped
    30ml/2 tbsp olive oil
    30ml/2 tbsp lemon juice
    good pinch of paprika
    pinch of ground cumin
    ¼ preserved lemon
    salt and ground black pepper
    fresh coriander (cilantro) and flat leaf
        parsley, to garnish

1 Preheat the grill (broiler) to its hottest setting. Grill (broil) the peppers skin side up until the skins are blackened, place in a plastic bag and tie the ends. Leave for about 10 minutes, until the peppers are cool enough to handle and then peel away and discard the skins.

2 Cut the peppers into small pieces, discarding the seeds and core, and place in a serving dish.

3 Peel the tomatoes by placing in boiling water for 1 minute, then plunging into cold water. Peel off the skins, then quarter them, discarding the core and seeds.

4 Chop the tomatoes roughly and add to the peppers. Scatter the chopped garlic on top and chill for 1 hour.

5 Whisk together the olive oil, lemon juice, paprika and cumin and pour over the salad. Season with salt and pepper.

6 Rinse the preserved lemon in cold water and remove the flesh and pith. Cut the peel into slivers and sprinkle over the salad. Garnish with coriander and flat leaf parsley.

Energy 100Kcal/423kJ; Protein 2.4g; Carbohydrate 9.1g, of which sugars 8.7g; Fat 6.5g, of which saturates 1.1g; Cholesterol 0mg; Calcium 24mg; Fibre 4.2g; Sodium 20mg.

PAN-FRIED BABY SQUID WITH SPICES

THIS DELICIOUS AND UNUSUAL DISH OF BABY SQUID IS A POPULAR CHOICE FOR AN APPETIZER IN AFRICA. IT NEEDS VERY LITTLE COOKING AND TASTES WONDERFUL WITH THIS SPICY SWEET AND SOUR SAUCE, WHICH TEAMS TURMERIC AND GINGER WITH HONEY AND LEMON JUICE.

SERVES FOUR

INGREDIENTS
   8 baby squid, prepared,
     with tentacles
   5ml/1 tsp ground turmeric
   15ml/1 tbsp smen or olive oil
   2 garlic cloves, finely chopped
   15g/½oz fresh root ginger, peeled
     and finely chopped
   5–10ml/1–2 tsp clear honey
   juice of 1 lemon
   10ml/2 tsp harissa
   salt
   small bunch of fresh coriander
     (cilantro), chopped, to garnish

1 Pat dry the squid bodies, inside and out, and dry the tentacles. Sprinkle the squid with the ground turmeric.

2 Heat the smen or olive oil in a large, heavy frying pan and stir in the garlic and ginger.

3 Just as the ginger and garlic begin to colour, add the squid and tentacles and fry quickly on both sides over a high heat. (Don't overcook the squid, otherwise it will become rubbery.)

4 Add the honey, lemon juice and harissa and stir to form a thick, spicy, caramelized sauce.

5 Season with salt, sprinkle with the chopped coriander and serve immediately.

COOK'S TIP
Smen is a pungent, aged butter used in Moroccan cooking. It is also savoured with chunks of warm, fresh bread and is used to enhance other dishes including couscous and some tagines.

Energy 154Kcal/647kJ; Protein 19.8g; Carbohydrate 5.8g, of which sugars 4.3g; Fat 5.9g, of which saturates 1g; Cholesterol 281mg; Calcium 54mg; Fibre 1g; Sodium 144mg.

HOT SPICY PRAWNS WITH CORIANDER

CORIANDER IS WIDELY GROWN AS A CASH CROP IN NORTH AFRICA, AND IT IS OFTEN USED TO FLAVOUR TAGINES AND SIMILAR DISHES. THE HERB'S AFFINITY FOR CUMIN IS WELL KNOWN, SO IT IS NOT SURPRISING TO FIND THE TWIN FLAVOURINGS USED IN THIS SPICY APPETIZER.

SERVES TWO TO FOUR

INGREDIENTS
60ml/4 tbsp olive oil
2–3 garlic cloves, chopped
25g/1oz fresh root ginger, peeled
  and grated
1 fresh red or green chilli, seeded
  and chopped
5ml/1 tsp cumin seeds
5ml/1 tsp paprika
450g/1lb uncooked king prawns
  (jumbo shrimp), shelled
bunch of fresh coriander
  (cilantro), chopped
salt
1 lemon, cut into wedges, to serve

1 In a large, frying pan, heat the oil with the garlic. Stir in the ginger, chilli and cumin seeds. Cook briefly, until the ingredients give off a lovely aroma, then add the paprika and toss in the prawns.

2 Fry the prawns over a fairly high heat, turning them frequently, for 3–5 minutes, until just cooked. Season to taste with salt and add the coriander. Serve immediately, with lemon wedges for squeezing over the prawns.

COOK'S TIP
When buying garlic, choose plump garlic with tightly packed cloves and dry skin. Avoid any bulbs with soft, shrivelled cloves or green shoots.

Energy 382Kcal/1591kJ; Protein 40.8g; Carbohydrate 1.1g, of which sugars 0.9g; Fat 23.9g, of which saturates 3.4g; Cholesterol 439mg; Calcium 254mg; Fibre 1.9g; Sodium 440mg.

MEAT BRIOUATES

THE MOROCCANS, WHO ENJOY THE TASTE OF SWEET AND SAVOURY TOGETHER, TRADITIONALLY SPRINKLE THESE LITTLE PASTRY SNACKS WITH GROUND CINNAMON AND ICING SUGAR. IT IS AN UNUSUAL BUT DELICIOUS COMBINATION.

MAKES ABOUT TWENTY-FOUR

INGREDIENTS
175g/6oz filo pastry sheets
40g/1½oz/3 tbsp butter, melted
sunflower oil, for frying
fresh flat leaf parsley, to garnish
ground cinnamon and icing
  (confectioners') sugar,
  to serve (optional)
For the meat filling
30ml/2 tbsp sunflower oil
1 onion, finely chopped
1 small bunch of fresh coriander
  (cilantro), chopped
1 small bunch of fresh
  parsley, chopped
375g/13oz lean minced (ground) beef
  or lamb
2.5ml/½ tsp paprika
5ml/1 tsp ground coriander
good pinch of ground ginger
2 eggs, beaten

1 First make the filling. Heat the oil in a frying pan and fry the onion and the chopped herbs over a low heat for about 4 minutes, until the onion is softened and translucent.

2 Add the meat to the frying pan and cook for about 5 minutes, stirring frequently, until the meat is evenly browned and most of the moisture has evaporated. Drain away any excess fat and stir in the spices.

3 Cook the spiced meat and onion for 1 minute, and then remove the pan from the heat and stir in the beaten eggs. Stir until they begin to set and resemble lightly scrambled eggs. Set aside.

4 Take a sheet of filo pastry and cut into 8.5cm/3½in strips. Cover the remaining pastry with clear film (plastic wrap) to prevent it drying out. Brush the pastry strip with melted butter, then place a heaped teaspoon of the meat filling about 1cm/½in from one end. Fold the corner over to make a triangle shape.

5 Fold the "triangle" over itself and then continue to fold, keeping the triangle shape, until you reach the end of the strip. Continue in this way until all the pastry and filling have been used up. You should make about 24 pastries.

6 Heat about 1cm/½in oil in a heavy pan and fry the briouates in batches for 2–3 minutes until golden, turning once. Drain on kitchen paper and arrange on a serving plate. Serve garnished with fresh parsley and sprinkled with ground cinnamon and icing sugar, if liked.

Energy 95Kcal/396kJ; Protein 4.2g; Carbohydrate 4.8g, of which sugars 0.5g; Fat 6.7g, of which saturates 2.3g; Cholesterol 29mg; Calcium 19mg; Fibre 0.4g; Sodium 30mg.

PRAWN BRIOUATES

IN MOROCCO, BRIOUATES ARE MADE WITH A SPECIAL PASTRY CALLED OUARKA. LIKE FILO, IT IS VERY THIN AND APT TO DRY OUT IF NOT KEPT COVERED. MAKING THE GENUINE ARTICLE IS TRICKY AND TAKES YEARS OF PRACTICE. FORTUNATELY FILO PASTRY MAKES A PERFECT SUBSTITUTE.

MAKES ABOUT TWENTY-FOUR

INGREDIENTS
175g/6oz filo pastry sheets
40g/1½oz/3 tbsp butter, melted
sunflower oil, for frying
1 spring onion (scallion) and fresh
   coriander (cilantro) leaves, to garnish
ground cinnamon and icing
   (confectioners') sugar, to serve
For the prawn (shrimp) filling
15ml/1 tbsp olive oil
15g/½oz/1 tbsp butter
2–3 spring onions (scallions),
   finely chopped
15g/½oz/2 tbsp plain (all-purpose) flour
300ml/½ pint/1¼ cups milk
2.5ml/½ tsp paprika
350g/12oz cooked peeled prawns
   (shrimp), chopped
salt and white pepper

1 First make the filling. Heat the olive oil and butter in a pan and fry the spring onions over a very gentle heat for 2–3 minutes until soft.

2 Stir in the flour, and then gradually add the milk. Heat gently, stirring continuously, until the sauce is thickened and smooth. Simmer gently for 2–3 minutes, stirring.

3 Season the sauce with paprika, salt and pepper and stir in the prawns.

COOK'S TIP
Chilled fresh or frozen filo pastry sheets are widely available from many supermarkets.

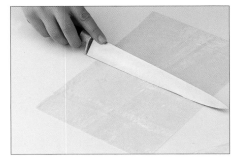

4 Take a sheet of filo pastry and cut it in half widthways, to make a rectangle about 18 x 14cm/7 x 5½in. Cover the remaining pastry with clear film (plastic wrap) to prevent it drying out.

5 Brush the pastry with melted butter and then place a heaped teaspoon of filling at one end of the pastry. Roll up like a cigar, tucking in the sides as you go. Continue in this way until you have used all the pastry and filling.

6 Heat about 1cm/½in oil in a heavy pan and fry the briouates, in batches if necessary, for 2–3 minutes until golden, turning occasionally. Drain on kitchen paper, arrange on a serving plate and then serve garnished with a spring onion and coriander leaves, and sprinkled with cinnamon and icing sugar, if liked.

Energy 77Kcal/320kJ; Protein 4.3g; Carbohydrate 5.5g, of which sugars 0.7g; Fat 4.3g, of which saturates 1.6g; Cholesterol 17mg; Calcium 47mg; Fibre 0.2g; Sodium 251mg.

SESAME-COATED MAJOUN

THE NOT-SO-SECRET INGREDIENT THAT TRADITIONALLY GIVES THESE SWEET AND SPICY SNACKS EXTRA FLAVOUR IS HASHISH. IT HAS BEEN OMITTED HERE, FOR OBVIOUS REASONS, BUT IS AS INTEGRAL TO THE GENUINE MOROCCAN RECIPE AS THE SPICES THAT FLAVOUR THE FRUIT, NUT AND HONEY MIX. MAJOUN, OFTEN CALLED HASHISH BALLS, ARE FAMED FOR THEIR NARCOTIC OR APHRODISIAC QUALITIES. THESE MAY NOT HAVE THE SAME EFFECT BUT ARE STILL DELICIOUS.

MAKES ABOUT TWENTY

INGREDIENTS
  500g/1¼lb/scant 3 cups
    blanched almonds
  250g/9oz/1½ cups walnuts
  500g/1¼lb/3⅓ cups raisins
  130g/4½oz/generous ½ cup butter
  250g/9oz/generous 1 cup clear honey
  7.5ml/1½ tsp ras el hanout
  7.5ml/1½ tsp ground ginger
  65–75g/2½–3oz sesame seeds

1 Finely chop the almonds, walnuts and raisins in a food processor or blender until they form a coarse, slightly sticky mixture. Alternatively, pound these ingredients together in batches in a large mortar using a pestle until the correct consistency is reached.

VARIATIONS
Use mixed spice (apple pie spice) or cinnamon in place of ginger. Use dried apricots in place of raisins.

2 Melt the butter in a large, heavy pan and stir in the honey, ras el hanout and ginger. Add the nuts and raisins and stir over a gentle heat for a few seconds until the mixture is thoroughly combined, firm and sticky.

3 Let the mixture cool a little, then shape into about 20 balls. Roll the balls in sesame seeds to coat completely. Serve warm or cold.

Energy 411Kcal/1711kJ; Protein 8.3g; Carbohydrate 29.1g, of which sugars 28.3g; Fat 29.8g, of which saturates 5.5g; Cholesterol 14mg; Calcium 107mg; Fibre 3g; Sodium 61mg.

TUNISIAN PLANTAIN SNACKS

SWEET AND CRISP, DEEP-FRIED SLICES OF PLAINTAIN ARE NOT ONLY A GREAT STREET SNACK, BUT ALSO MAKE EXCELLENT NIBBLES WITH DRINKS. THE SPICE MIXTURE USED HERE — ZAHTAR — IS POPULAR THROUGHOUT NORTH AFRICA. ITS BLEND OF SESAME SEEDS, SUMAC AND THYME IS PERFECT WITH PLANTAINS, AND THE CHILLI ADDS A WARM NOTE.

SERVES TWO TO FOUR AS A SNACK

INGREDIENTS
    2 large ripe plantains
    sunflower oil, for deep-frying
    1 dried red chilli, roasted, seeded
        and chopped
    15–30ml/1–2 tbsp zhatar
    coarse salt

1 To peel the plantains, cut off their ends with a sharp knife and make two or three incisions in the skin from end to end, then peel off the skin. Cut the plantains into thick slices.

2 Heat the oil for deep-frying in a heavy pan to 180°C/350°F, or until a cube of bread browns in 30–45 seconds. Fry the plantain slices in batches until golden brown. Drain each batch on a double layer of kitchen paper.

3 While still warm, place them in a shallow bowl and sprinkle liberally with the dried chilli, zahtar and salt. Toss them thoroughly and eat immediately.

COOK'S TIP
To roast the chilli, place the chilli in a small, heavy frying pan and cook over a medium heat, stirring constantly, until the chilli darkens and gives off a peppery aroma.

Energy 334Kcal/1408kJ; Protein 1.9g; Carbohydrate 59.4g, of which sugars 14.4g; Fat 11.5g, of which saturates 1.3g; Cholesterol 0mg; Calcium 8mg; Fibre 2.9g; Sodium 4mg.

YAM BALLS

MOST AFRICAN COUNTRIES HAVE A VERSION OF THIS POPULAR SNACK, MADE BY ROLLING A SPICY MIXTURE OF MASHED YAM AND VEGETABLES INTO BALLS, WHICH ARE THEN DEEP FRIED. THE SMOOTH TEXTURE OF THE MASHED YAM CONTRASTS BEAUTIFULLY WITH THE CHOPPED VEGETABLES.

MAKES ABOUT TWENTY-FOUR

INGREDIENTS
    450g/1lb white yam
    30ml/2 tbsp finely chopped onion
    45ml/3 tbsp chopped tomatoes
    2.5ml/½ tsp chopped fresh thyme
    1 fresh green chilli, finely chopped
    15ml/1 tbsp finely chopped
      spring onion (scallion)
    1 garlic clove, crushed
    1 egg, beaten
    salt and ground black pepper
    vegetable oil, for shallow frying
    seasoned flour, for dusting

COOK'S TIP
Add a selection of chopped fresh herbs
to the yam mixture; parsley, chives and
coriander (cilantro) make a good
combination. Mix in 30ml/2 tbsp with
the egg and seasoning.

1 Peel the yam, cut into pieces and boil
in salted water for about 30 minutes
until tender. Drain and mash.

2 Add the onion, tomatoes, thyme,
chilli, spring onion, garlic, then stir in
the egg and seasoning and mix well.

3 Using a dessertspoon, scoop a little of
the mixture at a time and with your
hands mould them into balls. Roll the
yam balls in the seasoned flour and set
aside until you have formed all the
mixture into balls.

4 Heat a little oil in a large frying pan,
and then fry the balls in batches for a
few minutes, until golden brown. Drain
the yam balls on kitchen paper and
keep them warm while cooking the rest
of the mixture. Serve hot.

TATALE

GHANAIANS WOULDN'T DREAM OF THROWING OVER-RIPE PLAINTAINS AWAY. INSTEAD, THEY MASH THEM WITH ONION, CHILLI AND FLOUR AND TRANSFORM THEM INTO THESE TASTY SNACKS.

SERVES FOUR

INGREDIENTS
    2 over-ripe plantains
    25–50g/1–2oz/¼–½ cup self-raising
      (self-rising) flour
    1 small onion, finely chopped
    1 egg, beaten
    5ml/1 tsp palm oil (optional)
    1 fresh green chilli, seeded
      and chopped
    salt
    vegetable oil, for shallow frying

1 Peel and mash the plantains. Place in
a bowl and add enough flour to bind,
stirring thoroughly.

2 Add the onion, egg, palm oil, if using,
chilli and salt. Mix well and then leave
to stand for 20 minutes.

3 Heat a little oil in a large frying pan.
Spoon dessertspoons of mixture into the
pan and fry in batches for 3–4 minutes
until golden, turning once. Drain the
fritters on kitchen paper and serve hot
or cold.

TOP Energy 179Kcal/754kJ; Protein 1.7g; Carbohydrate 31.8g, of which sugars 5.9g; Fat 5.9g, of which saturates 0.8g; Cholesterol 0mg; Calcium 21mg; Fibre 1.6g; Sodium 4mg.
BOTTOM Energy 47Kcal/195kJ; Protein 0.6g; Carbohydrate 5.6g, of which sugars 0.4g; Fat 2.6g, of which saturates 0.4g; Cholesterol 8mg; Calcium 5mg; Fibre 0.3g; Sodium 4mg.

TUNISIAN CHICKEN WINGS WITH ORANGES

THIS IS A GREAT RECIPE FOR THE BARBECUE — IT IS QUICK AND EASY TO PREPARE AND MAKES WONDERFUL FINGER FOOD. THE RUB THAT GIVES THE CHICKEN WINGS THEIR FIERY FLAVOUR IS BASED ON A CLASSIC TUNISIAN SPICE MIX CALLED HARISSA. TO BALANCE THE HEAT, ADD SEGMENTS OF BLOOD ORANGES, EITHER SERVED SEPARATELY OR COOKED ON SKEWERS WITH THE CHICKEN PORTIONS. CHERRY TOMATOES COULD BE USED INSTEAD OF THE ORANGES.

SERVES FOUR

INGREDIENTS
  60ml/4 tbsp fiery harissa
  30ml/2 tbsp olive oil
  16–20 chicken wings
  4 blood oranges, quartered
  icing (confectioners') sugar
  small bunch of fresh coriander
    (cilantro), chopped, to garnish
  salt

1 Preheat the grill (broiler) to its hottest setting. Put the harissa in a small bowl with the olive oil and mix to form a loose paste. Add a little salt and stir to combine.

2 Brush harissa mixture over the chicken wings so that they are well coated. Grill (broil) the wings for 5–8 minutes on each side, until cooked and a dark golden brown.

3 Once the wings begin to cook, dip the orange quarters lightly in icing sugar and grill them for a few minutes, until they are slightly burnt but not black and charred. Serve the chicken wings immediately with the oranges, sprinkled with a little chopped fresh coriander.

VARIATION
When blood oranges are out of season, normal oranges can be used instead.

Energy 500Kcal/2077kJ; Protein 44.8g; Carbohydrate 0g, of which sugars 0g; Fat 35.6g, of which saturates 8.9g; Cholesterol 196mg; Calcium 14mg; Fibre 0g; Sodium 132mg.

FISH AND CHERMOULA MINI PIES

THESE LITTLE SAVOURY PIES ARE MADE WITH THE MOROCCAN FINE PASTRY OUARKA, BUT FILO PASTRY WILL WORK JUST AS WELL. THE FILLING IS HIGHLY FLAVOURED WITH CHERMOULA, WHICH IS A MIXTURE OF SPICES AND MASSES OF FRESH CORIANDER AND FLAT LEAF PARSLEY. THE CHERMOULA MAY BE MADE IN ADVANCE AND STORED IN THE REFRIGERATOR FOR A FEW DAYS. YOU CAN VARY THE FILLING BY ADDING MUSSELS OR SCALLOPS, IF YOU LIKE.

MAKES EIGHT

INGREDIENTS
   500g/1¼lb firm white fish fillets
   225g/8oz uncooked king prawns
     (jumbo shrimp)
   16 sheets of ouarka or filo pastry
   60–75ml/4–5 tbsp sunflower oil
   1 egg yolk, mixed with a few drops
     of water
   salt
For the chermoula
   75ml/5 tbsp olive oil
   juice of 1 lemon
   5ml/1 tsp ground cumin
   5–10ml/1–2 tsp paprika
   2–3 garlic cloves, crushed
   1 red chilli, seeded and chopped
   large bunch of fresh flat leaf
     parsley, chopped
   large bunch of fresh coriander
     (cilantro), chopped

1 Prepare the chermoula. Combine all the ingredients in a bowl and set aside. Place the fish in a frying pan and add just enough water to cover the fillets.

2 Season the fish with a little salt and heat until just simmering, then cook gently for 3 minutes, until the fish just begins to flake. Use a slotted spoon to remove the fish from the liquid and break it up, taking care to remove all bones as you do so.

3 Poach the prawns in the fish liquor for 10 minutes, until they turn pink, then drain and shell them. Gently toss the prawns and fish in the chermoula, cover and set aside for 1 hour.

4 Preheat the oven to 180°C/350°F/ Gas 4 and grease two baking sheets. To make the pies, lay the filo pastry under a damp cloth. Take two sheets of filo: brush one with oil, lay the second one on top, then brush it with oil.

5 Place some of the fish mixture in the middle of the length of the sheet but to one side of its width. Fold the edge of the pastry over the filling, then fold the long side over to cover the filling.

VARIATION
Instead of neat parcels, the filo and filling can be shaped into open boats or slipper shapes, as shown below.

6 Wrap the ends of the pastry around the filling like a collar to make a neat package with the edges tucked in, then brush with egg yolk.

7 Continue as before with the rest of the fish and chermoula mixture. Bake the pies for about 20 minutes, until the pastry is crisp and golden brown. Serve hot or warm.

Energy 236Kcal/984kJ; Protein 18.2g; Carbohydrate 10g, of which sugars 0.4g; Fat 13.9g, of which saturates 2g; Cholesterol 109mg; Calcium 67mg; Fibre 0.9g; Sodium 96mg.

MAIN COURSES

Africans have a vast store of fish, meat and chicken recipes, but often prefer the simplest methods of cooking and grilling, especially over an open fire. This chapter shows the different approaches adopted by cooks from these regions. You'll find sweet and fruity tagines from Morocco, mouthwatering North African stews, which are cooked in distinctive dishes, to rib-sticking ragouts favoured by Nigerian cooks.

FISH WITH CRAB MEAT AND AUBERGINE

IN MAURITIUS, HOME OF THE FAMOUS BLUE SWIMMER CRABS AND SAND CRABS, THIS SHELLFISH IS VERY POPULAR. COMBINING IT WITH SALMON AND AUBERGINE CREATES A SOPHISTICATED DISH.

SERVES FOUR

INGREDIENTS

450–675g/1–1½lb salmon fillet,
  skinned and cut into 4 pieces
2 garlic cloves, crushed
juice of ½ lemon
15ml/1 tbsp vegetable oil
15g/½oz/1 tbsp butter or margarine
1 onion, cut into rings
175g/6oz fresh or canned crab meat
salt and ground black pepper
For the aubergine (eggplant) sauce
  25g/1oz/2 tbsp butter or margarine
  30ml/2 tbsp chopped spring onion
    (scallion)
  2 tomatoes, skinned and chopped
  ½ red (bell) pepper, seeded and
    finely chopped
  1 large aubergine (eggplant), peeled
    and chopped
  450ml/¾ pint/scant 2 cups fish or
    vegetable stock
  salt and ground black pepper

1 Place the salmon fillet in a shallow, non-metallic dish, season with the garlic and a little salt and pepper. Sprinkle with the lemon juice, cover loosely with clear film (plastic wrap) and set aside to marinate in a cool place for 1 hour.

2 Meanwhile, make the aubergine sauce. Melt the butter or margarine in a pan and gently fry the spring onion and tomatoes for 5 minutes.

3 Add the red pepper and aubergine, stir together and then add 300ml/ ½ pint/1¼ cups of the stock. Simmer for 20 minutes, until the aubergines are mushy and the liquid has been absorbed and then mash the mixture together well with a fork.

4 To cook the salmon, heat the oil and butter or margarine in a large frying pan. When the butter has melted, scatter the onion rings over the bottom of the pan and lay the salmon pieces on top. Cover each piece of salmon with crab meat and then spoon the aubergine mixture on top.

5 Pour the remaining stock around the salmon, cover with a lid and cook over a low to moderate heat, until the salmon is cooked through and flakes easily when tested with a knife. The sauce should be thick and fairly dry.

6 Arrange the fish on warmed serving plates, spoon extra sauce over and serve at once.

COOK'S TIP
Use a fish slice or metal spatula to carefully transfer the salmon fillet to serving plates, to prevent breaking up the fish.

Energy 372Kcal/1548kJ; Protein 32.4g; Carbohydrate 6.5g, of which sugars 5.8g; Fat 24.3g, of which saturates 7.9g; Cholesterol 109mg; Calcium 98mg; Fibre 3.1g; Sodium 360mg.

SPICY SHELLFISH COUSCOUS

THIS IS PRECISELY THE TYPE OF DISH YOU MIGHT ENJOY ON A WARM EVENING AT A BEACH BAR IN CASABLANCA OR TANGIER. THE COUSCOUS IS FLAVOURED WITH HARISSA, A SPICY CHILLI PASTE, BEFORE BEING BAKED IN THE OVEN. IT IS TOPPED WITH MUSSELS AND PRAWNS AND MOISTENED WITH A MARVELLOUSLY CREAMY SAUCE, WHICH JUST BEGS TO BE MOPPED UP WITH BREAD.

SERVES FOUR TO SIX

INGREDIENTS
  500g/1¼lb/3 cups couscous
  5ml/1 tsp salt
  600ml/1 pint/2½ cups warm water
  45ml/3 tbsp sunflower oil
  5–10ml/1–2 tsp harissa
  25g/1oz/2 tbsp butter, diced
For the shellfish broth
  500g/1¼lb mussels in their shells,
    scrubbed, with beards removed
  500g/1¼lb uncooked prawns
    (shrimp) in their shells
  juice of 1 lemon
  50g/2oz/¼ cup butter
  2 shallots, finely chopped
  5ml/1 tsp coriander seeds, roasted
    and ground
  5ml/1 tsp cumin seeds, roasted
    and ground
  2.5ml/½ tsp ground turmeric
  2.5ml/½ tsp cayenne pepper
  5–10ml/1–2 tsp plain
    (all-purpose) flour
  600ml/1 pint/2½ cups fish stock
  120ml/4fl oz/½ cup double
    (heavy) cream
  salt and ground black pepper
  small bunch of fresh coriander
    (cilantro), finely chopped

COOK'S TIP
To roast spices, toss the spices in a heavy pan over a high heat until they begin to change colour and give off a nutty aroma, then tip them into a bowl.

1 Preheat the oven to 180°C/350°F/ Gas 4. Place the couscous in a bowl. Stir the salt into the warm water, then pour over the couscous, stirring. Set aside for 10 minutes.

2 Stir the sunflower oil into the harissa to make a paste, then, using your fingers, rub it into the couscous and break up any lumps. Tip into an ovenproof dish, arrange the butter over the top, cover with foil and cook in the oven for about 20 minutes.

3 Meanwhile, put the mussels and prawns in a pan, add the lemon juice and 50ml/2fl oz/¼ cup water, cover and cook for 3–4 minutes, shaking the pan, until the mussels have opened. Drain the shellfish, reserving the liquor, and discard any closed mussels.

4 Heat the butter in a large pan. Cook the shallots for 5 minutes, or until softened. Add the spices and fry for 1 minute. Off the heat, stir in the flour, the fish stock and shellfish cooking liquor. Bring to the boil, stirring. Add the cream and simmer, stirring occasionally, for about 10 minutes. Season with salt and pepper.

5 Shell about two-thirds of the mussels and prawns, then add the shellfish and most of the fresh coriander to the pan. Heat through, then sprinkle with the remaining coriander.

6 Fluff up the couscous with a fork or your fingers, working in the melted butter. To serve, pass round the couscous and ladle the broth over the top.

Energy 734Kcal/3050kJ; Protein 24.5g; Carbohydrate 67.1g, of which sugars 1.5g; Fat 42.3g, of which saturates 21g; Cholesterol 223mg; Calcium 113mg; Fibre 0.2g; Sodium 360mg.

TAGINE OF MONKFISH

THE FISH IS MARINATED IN CHERMOULA, A LEMONY GARLIC AND CORIANDER PASTE, WHICH GIVES IT THAT UNMISTAKABLE MOROCCAN FLAVOUR. MONKFISH IS ROBUST ENOUGH TO HOLD ITS OWN AGAINST THE SPICES AND BLACK OLIVES, AND THE RESULT IS A VERY TASTY DISH. IT DOESN'T REALLY NEED BREAD, AS POTATOES ARE INCLUDED, BUT YOU MAY NOT BE ABLE TO RESIST MOPPING UP THE JUICES.

SERVES FOUR

INGREDIENTS
  900g/2lb monkfish tail, cut
    into chunks
  15–20 small new potatoes, scrubbed,
    scraped or peeled
  45–60ml/3–4 tbsp olive oil
  4–5 garlic cloves, thinly sliced
  15–20 cherry tomatoes
  2 green (bell) peppers, grilled
    (broiled) until black, skinned,
    seeded and cut into strips
  large handful of kalamata or fleshy
    black olives
  about 100ml/3½fl oz/scant ½ cup
    water
  salt and ground black pepper
For the chermoula
  2 garlic cloves
  5ml/1 tsp coarse salt
  10ml/2 tsp ground cumin
  5ml/1 tsp paprika
  juice of 1 lemon
  small bunch of fresh coriander
    (cilantro), roughly chopped
  15ml/1 tbsp olive oil

1 Use a mortar and pestle to make the chermoula: pound the garlic with the salt to a smooth paste. Add the cumin, paprika, lemon juice and chopped coriander, and gradually mix in the oil to emulsify the mixture slightly.

2 Reserve a little chermoula for cooking, then rub the rest of the paste over the monkfish. Cover and leave to marinate in a cool place for 1 hour.

3 Par-boil the potatoes for about 10 minutes. Drain, then cut them in half lengthways. Heat the olive oil in a heavy pan and stir in the garlic. When the garlic begins to colour, add the tomatoes and cook until just softened.

4 Add the peppers to the tomatoes and garlic, together with the remaining chermoula, and season to taste.

5 Spread the potatoes over the base of a tagine, shallow pan or deep, ridged frying pan. Spoon three-quarters of the tomato and pepper mixture over and place the marinated fish chunks on top, with their marinade.

6 Spoon the rest of the tomato and pepper mixture on top of the fish and add the olives. Drizzle a little extra olive oil over the dish and pour in the water.

7 Heat until simmering, cover the tagine or pan with a lid and cook over a medium heat for about 15 minutes, until the fish is cooked through. Serve with fresh, warm crusty bread to mop up the delicious juices.

Energy 406Kcal/1710kJ; Protein 39.6g; Carbohydrate 25.2g, of which sugars 6.5g; Fat 17.1g, of which saturates 2.7g; Cholesterol 32mg; Calcium 98mg; Fibre 5.4g; Sodium 915mg.

RED MULLET WITH CHERMOULA

THE CORIANDER AND CHILLI CHERMOULA MARINADE GIVES THIS DISH ITS DISTINCT FLAVOUR. THE OLIVES AND PRESERVED LEMON ADD A TOUCH OF EXCITEMENT. ON THEIR OWN, THESE MULLET MAKE A DELICIOUS APPETIZER. SERVED WITH SAFFRON COUSCOUS AND A CRISP, HERB-FILLED SALAD, THEY ARE DELICIOUS AS A MAIN COURSE. CHOOSE LARGER FISH IF YOU WISH.

SERVES FOUR

INGREDIENTS
    30–45ml/2–3 tbsp olive oil, plus
      extra for brushing
    1 onion, chopped
    1 carrot, chopped
    ½ preserved lemon, finely chopped
    4 plum tomatoes, skinned
      and chopped
    600ml/1 pint/2½ cups fish stock
      or water
    3–4 new potatoes, peeled and diced
    4 small red mullet or snapper, gutted
      and filleted
    handful of black olives, pitted
      and halved
    small bunch of fresh coriander
      (cilantro), chopped
    small bunch of fresh mint, chopped
    salt and ground black pepper
For the chermoula
    small bunch of fresh coriander
      (cilantro), finely chopped
    2–3 garlic cloves, chopped
    5–10ml/1–2 tsp ground cumin
    pinch of saffron threads
    60ml/4 tbsp olive oil
    juice of 1 lemon
    1 hot red chilli, seeded and chopped
    5ml/1 tsp salt

1 To make the chermoula, pound the ingredients in a mortar with a pestle, or process them together in a food processor, then set aside.

2 Heat the olive oil in a pan. Add the onion and carrot and cook until softened but not browned. Stir in half the preserved lemon, along with 30ml/ 2 tbsp of the chermoula, the tomatoes and the stock or water.

3 Bring to the boil, then reduce the heat, cover and simmer gently for about 30 minutes. Add the potatoes and simmer for a further 10 minutes, until they are tender.

4 Preheat the grill (broiler) on the hottest setting and brush a baking sheet or grill pan with oil. Brush the fish fillets with olive oil and a little chermoula. Season with salt and pepper, then place skin side up, on the sheet or pan and cook under the grill for 5–6 minutes.

5 Meanwhile, stir the olives, the remaining chermoula and preserved lemon into the sauce and check the seasoning. Serve the fish fillets in wide bowls, spoon the sauce over and sprinkle liberally with chopped coriander and mint.

Energy 374Kcal/1558kJ; Protein 24.7g; Carbohydrate 13.8g, of which sugars 7.2g; Fat 24.9g, of which saturates 2.9g; Cholesterol 0mg; Calcium 193mg; Fibre 4.7g; Sodium 704mg.

YELLOWTAIL WITH LEMON AND RED ONION

THIS DELICIOUS GAME FISH IS FOUND IN SOUTH AFRICAN WATERS, THE FLESH CAN BE DRY, BUT SIMMERING IT IN STOCK KEEPS IT BEAUTIFULLY MOIST. HALIBUT OR COD CAN BE SUBSTITUTED.

SERVES FOUR

INGREDIENTS

4 yellowtail, halibut or cod steaks or
  cutlets, about 175g/6oz each
juice of 1 lemon
5ml/1 tsp garlic powder
5ml/1 tsp paprika
5ml/1 tsp ground cumin
4ml/¾ tsp dried tarragon
about 60ml/4 tbsp olive oil
plain (all-purpose) flour, for dusting
300ml/½ pint/1¼ cups fish stock
2 fresh red chillies, seeded and
  finely chopped
30ml/2 tbsp chopped fresh
  coriander (cilantro)
1 red onion, cut into rings
salt and ground black pepper

1 Place the fish in a shallow, non-metallic bowl. Mix together the lemon juice, garlic powder, paprika, cumin, tarragon, salt and pepper. Spoon over the fish, cover with clear film (plastic wrap) and leave overnight in the fridge.

2 Gently heat the oil in a large frying pan, dust the fish with flour and then fry on each side, until golden brown.

3 Pour the fish stock around the fish, and simmer, covered, for about 5 minutes, until the fish is almost cooked through.

4 Add the red chillies and 15ml/1 tbsp of the chopped coriander to the pan. Simmer for a further 5 minutes.

5 Transfer the fish and sauce to a serving plate and keep warm.

6 Wipe the pan, heat some olive oil in the pan and stir-fry the onion rings until speckled brown. Scatter over the fish with the remaining chopped coriander and serve at once.

Energy 265Kcal/1106kJ; Protein 33g; Carbohydrate 5.4g, of which sugars 1.2g; Fat 12.5g, of which saturates 1.8g; Cholesterol 81mg; Calcium 47mg; Fibre 0.9g; Sodium 109mg.

TANZANIAN FRIED FISH WITH COCONUT

A SPINACH AND COCONUT MILK SAUCE, STUDDED WITH PRAWNS AND RED CHILLI, LOOKS VERY PRETTY WHEN PUDDLED AROUND GOUJONS OF FRIED FISH THAT HAVE BEEN MARINATED IN SPICES.

SERVES FOUR

INGREDIENTS

450g/1lb white fish fillets (cod or haddock)
15ml/1 tbsp lemon or lime juice
2.5ml/½ tsp garlic powder
5ml/1 tsp ground cinnamon
2.5ml/½ tsp dried thyme
2.5ml/½ tsp paprika
2.5ml/½ tsp ground black pepper
seasoned flour, for dusting
vegetable oil, for shallow frying
salt

For the sauce

25g/1oz/2 tbsp butter or margarine
1 onion, finely chopped
1 garlic clove, crushed
300ml/½ pint/1¼ cups coconut milk
115g/4oz fresh spinach, thinly sliced
225–275g/8–10oz cooked, peeled prawns (shrimp)
1 fresh red chilli, seeded and finely chopped

1 Place the fish fillets in a shallow bowl or non-metallic dish and sprinkle with the lemon or lime juice.

2 Blend together the garlic powder, cinnamon, thyme, paprika, black pepper and salt and sprinkle over the fish. Cover loosely with clear film (plastic wrap) and leave to marinate in a cool place or refrigerator for a few hours.

3 Meanwhile, make the sauce. Melt the butter or margarine in a large pan and fry the onion and garlic for 5–6 minutes, until the onion is soft, stirring frequently.

4 Place the coconut milk and spinach in a separate pan and bring to the boil. Cook gently for a few minutes until the spinach has wilted and the coconut milk has reduced a little, then remove from the heat and set aside to cool slightly.

5 Process the spinach mixture in a blender or food processor for 30 seconds then add to the onion with the prawns and red chilli. Stir well and simmer gently for a few minutes then set aside while cooking the fish.

6 Cut the marinated fish into 5cm/2in pieces and dip in the seasoned flour. Heat a little oil in a large frying pan and fry the fish pieces, in batches if necessary, for 2–3 minutes each side, until golden brown. Drain on kitchen paper.

7 Arrange the fish on a warmed serving plate. Gently reheat the sauce and serve separately in a sauce boat or poured over the fish.

VARIATION
Use 1 clove crushed fresh garlic in place of garlic powder.

Energy 259Kcal/1087kJ; Protein 32.5g; Carbohydrate 5.4g, of which sugars 5g; Fat 12.1g, of which saturates 4.3g; Cholesterol 164mg; Calcium 136mg; Fibre 0.8g; Sodium 343mg.

TANZANIAN FISH CURRY

WITH LAKES ON ITS WESTERN AND NORTHERN BORDERS, AND THE SEA TO THE EAST, TANZANIA HAS A RICH INSPIRATION FOR ITS FISH DISHES. THIS SIMPLE TREATMENT OF SNAPPER OR BREAM WORKS WELL.

SERVES TWO TO THREE

INGREDIENTS

    1 large snapper or red bream
    1 lemon
    45ml/3 tbsp vegetable oil
    1 onion, finely chopped
    2 garlic cloves, crushed
    45ml/3 tbsp curry powder
    400g/14oz can chopped tomatoes
    20ml/1 heaped tbsp smooth peanut
      butter, preferably unsalted
    ½ green (bell) pepper, seeded
      and chopped
    2 slices fresh root ginger, chopped
    1 fresh green chilli, seeded and
      finely chopped
    about 600ml/1 pint/2½ cups
      fish stock
    15ml/1 tbsp finely chopped fresh
      coriander (cilantro)
    salt and ground black pepper

1 Season the fish with salt and pepper and squeeze half a lemon over it. Cover, and leave in a cool place for 2 hours.

2 Heat the oil in a pan and fry the onion and garlic for 5–6 minutes. Reduce the heat, add the curry powder and stir in.

3 Stir in the tomatoes and then the peanut butter, mixing well, then add the green pepper, ginger, chilli and stock. Stir well and simmer gently for 10 minutes.

COOK'S TIP
The fish can be fried before adding to the sauce, if preferred. Dip in seasoned flour and fry in oil in a pan or a wok for a few minutes before adding to the sauce.

4 Cut the fish into pieces and gently lower into the sauce. Simmer for a further 20 minutes or until the fish is cooked, then using a slotted spoon, transfer the fish pieces to a plate.

5 Stir the coriander into the sauce and adjust the seasoning. If the sauce is very thick, add a little stock or water. Return the fish to the sauce, heat through and then serve immediately.

Energy 483Kcal/2020kJ; Protein 44.5g; Carbohydrate 12.8g, of which sugars 10.9g; Fat 28.7g, of which saturates 3.7g; Cholesterol 86mg; Calcium 129mg; Fibre 3.2g; Sodium 364mg.

KING PRAWNS IN ALMOND SAUCE

A DELECTABLE SEAFOOD CURRY FROM MAURITIUS, WHERE THE PRAWNS ARE LARGE AND SUCCULENT AND CHRISTOPHENE — OR CHO-CHO AS IT'S LOCALLY KNOWN — IS A POPULAR VEGETABLE.

SERVES FOUR

INGREDIENTS
   450g/1lb raw king prawns
      (jumbo shrimp)
   600ml/1 pint/2½ cups water
   3 thin slices fresh root ginger, peeled
   10ml/2 tsp curry powder
   2 garlic cloves, crushed
   15g/½oz/1 tbsp butter or margarine
   60ml/4 tbsp ground almonds
   1 fresh green chilli, seeded and
      finely chopped
   45ml/3 tbsp single (light) cream
   salt and ground black pepper
For the vegetables
   15ml/1 tbsp mustard oil
   15ml/1 tbsp vegetable oil
   1 onion, sliced
   ½ red (bell) pepper, seeded and
      thinly sliced
   ½ green (bell) pepper, seeded and
      thinly sliced
   1 christophene, peeled, stoned
      (pitted) and cut into strips

1 Shell the prawns and place the shells in a pan with the water and ginger. Simmer, uncovered, for 15 minutes until reduced by half. Strain into a jug (pitcher), discard the shells and ginger.

2 De-vein the prawns, place in a bowl and season with the curry powder, garlic and salt and pepper and set aside.

3 Heat the mustard and vegetable oils in a large frying pan, add the vegetables and stir-fry for 5 minutes. Season, spoon into a dish and keep warm.

4 Wipe out the frying pan, then melt the butter or margarine in the pan and sauté the prawns for about 5 minutes, until pink. Spoon over the bed of vegetables, cover and keep warm.

5 Add the ground almonds and chilli to the pan, stir-fry for a few seconds and then add the reserved stock and bring to the boil. Reduce the heat, stir in the cream and cook for a few minutes, without boiling. Pour the sauce over the vegetables and prawns before serving.

FRIED POMFRET IN COCONUT SAUCE

POMFRET ARE FOUND IN THE MEDITERRANEAN, BUT THE BEST-FLAVOURED FISH COME FROM THE INDIAN OCEAN. THIS IS HOW IT IS COOKED IN ZANZIBAR.

SERVES FOUR

INGREDIENTS
   4 medium pomfret
   juice of 1 lemon
   5ml/1 tsp garlic powder
   salt and ground black pepper
   vegetable oil, for shallow frying
For the coconut sauce
   450ml/¾ pint/scant 2 cups water
   2 thin slices fresh root ginger, peeled
   25–40g/1–1½oz creamed coconut or
      60–90ml/4–6 tbsp coconut cream
   30ml/2 tbsp vegetable oil
   1 red onion, sliced
   2 garlic cloves, crushed
   1 green chilli, seeded and sliced
   15ml/1 tbsp chopped fresh
      coriander (cilantro)

1 Cut the fish in half and sprinkle with the lemon juice. Season with garlic powder, salt and pepper and marinate in a cool place for a few hours.

2 Heat a little oil in a large frying pan. Pat the fish dry, fry in the oil for 10 minutes, turning once. Set aside.

3 To make the sauce, place the water in a pan with the slices of ginger, bring to the boil and simmer until the liquid is reduced to just over 300ml/½ pint/ 1¼ cups. Remove the ginger and reserve, then add the creamed coconut or coconut cream to the pan and stir until the coconut has melted.

4 Heat the oil in a wok or large pan and fry the onion and garlic for 2–3 minutes. Add the reserved ginger and coconut stock, the chilli and chopped coriander, stir well and then gently add the fish. Simmer for 10 minutes, until the fish is cooked through. Transfer the fish to a warmed serving plate, adjust the seasoning for the sauce and pour over the fish. Serve immediately.

TOP Energy 301Kcal/1251kJ; Protein 24.3g; Carbohydrate 6.1g, of which sugars 5.1g; Fat 20.1g, of which saturates 4.8g; Cholesterol 234mg; Calcium 154mg; Fibre 2.4g; Sodium 244mg.
BOTTOM Energy 210Kcal/875kJ; Protein 23.2g; Carbohydrate 2.3g, of which sugars 2g; Fat 12g, of which saturates 1.5g; Cholesterol 58mg; Calcium 23mg; Fibre 0.2g; Sodium 101mg.

Nigerian Lobster Piri Piri

Dried shrimps intensify the flavour of this seafood dish. The sauce uses easy-to-obtain ingredients like onions, tomatoes and chilli, with chopped ginger for added piquancy.

SERVES TWO TO FOUR

INGREDIENTS
    60ml/4 tbsp vegetable oil
    2 onions, chopped
    5ml/1 tsp chopped fresh root ginger
    450g/1lb fresh or canned
      tomatoes, chopped
    15ml/1 tbsp tomato purée (paste)
    225g/8oz cooked, peeled
      prawns (shrimp)
    10ml/2 tsp ground coriander
    1 green chilli, seeded and chopped
    15ml/1 tbsp dried shrimps, ground
    600ml/1 pint/2½ cups water
    1 green (bell) pepper, seeded
      and sliced
    2 cooked lobsters, halved
    salt and ground black pepper
    fresh coriander (cilantro) sprigs,
      to garnish

1 Heat the oil in a large, flameproof casserole and fry the onions, ginger, tomatoes and tomato purée for 5 minutes, until the onions are soft. Add the prawns, ground coriander, chilli and ground shrimps and stir well to mix.

2 Stir in the water, green pepper and salt and pepper, bring to the boil and simmer, uncovered, over a medium heat for about 20–30 minutes, until the sauce is reduced.

3 Add the lobsters to the sauce and cook for a few minutes to heat through. Arrange the lobster halves on warmed serving plates and pour the sauce over each one. Garnish with coriander sprigs and serve with fluffy white rice.

VARIATION
Use ground dried crayfish in place of ground dried shrimps, if preferred.

Energy 588Kcal/2464kJ; Protein 64.9g; Carbohydrate 24.5g, of which sugars 20.4g; Fat 26.6g, of which saturates 3.3g; Cholesterol 419mg; Calcium 270mg; Fibre 5.1g; Sodium 918mg.

NIGERIAN MEAT STEW

LIFT THE LID ON A NIGERIAN COOKING POT AND YOU WILL GENERALLY FIND A STEW INSIDE, WHICH WILL HAVE BEEN INSPIRED BY WHATEVER INGREDIENTS WERE AVAILABLE AT MARKET THAT DAY — A SINGLE TYPE OF MEAT OR A MIXTURE, PLUS VEGETABLES. OCCASIONALLY NIGERIAN WOMEN WILL ADD DRIED FISH OR SNAILS TO MEAT STEWS.

SERVES FOUR TO SIX

INGREDIENTS
    675g/1½lb oxtail, chopped
    450g/1lb stewing beef, cubed
    450g/1lb skinless, chicken breast
        fillets, diced
    2 garlic cloves, crushed
    1½ onions
    30ml/2 tbsp palm or vegetable oil
    30ml/2 tbsp tomato purée (paste)
    400g/14oz can plum tomatoes
    2 bay leaves
    5ml/1 tsp dried thyme
    5ml/1 tsp mixed spice (apple pie
        spice)
    salt and ground black pepper

1 Place the oxtail in a large pan, cover with water and bring to the boil. Skim the surface of any froth, then cover and cook for 1½ hours, adding more water as necessary. Add the beef and continue to cook for a further 1 hour.

2 Meanwhile, season the chicken with the crushed garlic and roughly chop one of the onions.

3 Heat the oil in a large pan over a medium heat and fry the chopped onion for about 5 minutes, until soft.

4 Stir the tomato purée in to the onions, cook briskly for a few minutes, then add the chicken. Stir well and cook gently for 5 minutes.

5 Meanwhile, place the plum tomatoes and the remaining half onion in a blender or food processor and process to a purée. Stir into the chicken mixture with the bay leaves, thyme, mixed spice and seasoning.

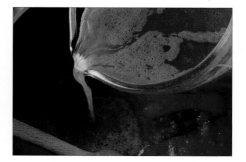

6 Add about 600ml/1 pint/2½ cups of stock from the cooked oxtail and beef and simmer for 35 minutes.

7 Add the oxtail and beef to the chicken. Heat gently, adjust the seasoning and serve hot.

Energy 588Kcal/2472kJ; Protein 88.3g; Carbohydrate 8.8g, of which sugars 7.2g; Fat 22.5g, of which saturates 9g; Cholesterol 281mg; Calcium 56mg; Fibre 1.8g; Sodium 390mg.

BEEF KOFTA CURRY

KOFTAS COME IN VARIOUS SHAPES AND SIZES. THE BASIC MINCED MEAT MIXTURE CAN BE MOULDED AROUND A SKEWER, SAUSAGE-STYLE, OR SHAPED INTO MEATBALLS. IN THIS VARIATION, THE MORE COMMONLY USED LAMB IS REPLACED BY BEEF, WHICH WORKS WELL WITH THE HOT CURRY SAUCE.

SERVES FOUR

INGREDIENTS
For the meatballs
   450g/1lb minced (ground) beef
   45ml/3 tbsp finely chopped onion
   15ml/1 tbsp chopped fresh
    coriander (cilantro)
   15ml/1 tbsp natural (plain) yogurt
   about 60ml/4 tbsp plain
    (all-purpose) flour
   10ml/2 tsp ground cumin
   5ml/1 tsp garam masala
   5ml/1 tsp ground turmeric
   5ml/1 tsp ground coriander
   1 fresh green chilli, seeded and
    finely chopped
   2 garlic cloves, crushed
   1.5ml/¼ tsp black mustard seeds
   1 egg (optional)
   salt and ground black pepper
For the curry sauce
   30ml/2 tbsp butter
   1 onion, finely chopped
   2 garlic cloves, crushed
   45ml/3 tbsp curry powder
   4 green cardamom pods
   600ml/1 pint/2½ cups hot beef stock
    or water
   15ml/1 tbsp tomato purée (paste)
   30ml/2 tbsp natural (plain) yogurt
   15ml/1 tbsp chopped fresh
    coriander (cilantro)

1 To make the meatballs, put the beef into a large bowl, add all the remaining meatball ingredients and mix well with your hands. Roll the mixture into small balls or koftas and then put aside on a floured plate until required.

2 To make the curry sauce, heat the butter in a pan over a medium heat and fry the onion and garlic for about 10 minutes, until the onion is soft.

3 Reduce the heat and then add the curry powder and cardamon pods and cook for a few minutes, stirring well.

4 Slowly stir in the stock or water and then add the tomato purée, yogurt and chopped coriander and stir well.

5 Simmer gently for 10 minutes. Add the koftas a few at a time, allow to cook briefly and then add a few more, until all of the koftas are in the pan. Simmer, uncovered, for about 20 minutes, until the koftas are cooked through. Avoid stirring, but gently shake the pan occasionally to move the koftas around. The curry should thicken slightly but if it becomes too dry, add a little more stock or water. Serve hot.

Energy 313Kcal/1301kJ; Protein 25.8g; Carbohydrate 4.9g, of which sugars 3.7g; Fat 21.3g, of which saturates 11.3g; Cholesterol 90mg; Calcium 42mg; Fibre 1g; Sodium 192mg.

GAMBIAN BEEF IN AUBERGINE SAUCE

BEEF IS POPULAR IN THE GAMBIA. IT IS RELATIVELY EXPENSIVE, THOUGH, SO IS USUALLY RESERVED FOR SPECIAL OCCASION DISHES LIKE THIS MILDLY SPICED AUBERGINE AND BEEF STEW.

SERVES FOUR

INGREDIENTS

450g/1lb stewing beef, cubed
5ml/1 tsp dried thyme
45ml/3 tbsp palm or vegetable oil
1 large onion, finely chopped
2 garlic cloves, crushed
4 canned plum tomatoes, chopped,
  plus the juice
15ml/1 tbsp tomato purée (paste)
2.5ml/½ tsp mixed spice (apple pie
  spice)
1 fresh red chilli, seeded and
  finely chopped
900ml/1½ pints/3¾ cups beef stock
1 large aubergine (eggplant), about
  350g/12oz
salt and ground black pepper

4 Simmer for 5–10 minutes, stirring occasionally. Stir in the tomato purée, mixed spice, chilli and remaining thyme, and then add the reserved beef and stock. Bring to the boil, cover and simmer for 30 minutes.

5 Cut the aubergine into 1cm/½in dice. Stir into the beef mixture and cook, covered, for a further 30 minutes, until the beef is completely tender. Adjust the seasoning and serve hot.

1 Season the cubed beef with 2.5ml/½ tsp thyme, salt and pepper.

2 Heat 15ml/1 tbsp of the oil in a pan and fry the meat for 8–10 minutes, until browned. Transfer to a bowl and set aside. Add the remaining oil to the pan.

3 Fry the onion and garlic for a few minutes, then add the tomatoes.

Energy 251Kcal/1050kJ; Protein 27.2g; Carbohydrate 7.2g, of which sugars 6.2g; Fat 12.8g, of which saturates 2.9g; Cholesterol 75mg; Calcium 29mg; Fibre 3g; Sodium 87mg.

AWAZE TIBS

An Ethiopian dish, Awaze Tibs is flavoured with berbere, a powerful blend of chillies with local herbs and spices. This version offers alternative flavourings that are more readily available, but for a truly authentic taste, look out for the packaged spice mix.

SERVES FOUR

INGREDIENTS
   450g/1lb lamb fillet
   45ml/3 tbsp olive oil
   1 red onion, sliced
   2.5ml/½ tsp peeled, grated fresh
      root ginger
   2 garlic cloves, crushed
   ½ fresh green chilli, seeded and
      finely chopped (optional)
   15ml/1 tbsp clarified butter or ghee
   salt and ground black pepper
For the berbere
   2.5ml/½ tsp each chilli powder,
      paprika, ground ginger, ground
      cinnamon, ground cardamom seeds
      and dried basil
   5ml/1 tsp garlic powder

1 To make the berbere, combine all the ingredients in a small bowl and tip into an airtight container. Berbere will keep for several months if stored in a cool, dry place.

2 Trim the lamb of any fat and then cut the meat into 2cm/¾in cubes.

3 Heat the oil in a large frying pan and fry the meat and onion for 5–6 minutes, until the meat is browned on all sides, stirring occasionally.

4 Add the ginger and garlic to the pan, together with 10ml/2 tsp of the berbere, then stir-fry over a brisk heat for a further 5–10 minutes.

5 Add the chilli, if using, and season well with salt and pepper. Just before serving, add the butter or ghee and stir well.

COOK'S TIPS
Clarified butter is traditionally used for this recipe. It can be made by gently heating butter, preferably unsalted (sweet) butter, up to boiling point and then scooping off and discarding the milk solids that rise to the surface. You are then left with clarified butter, which is a clear yellow liquid. Ghee is an Indian version of clarified butter which is made by simmering butter until all the moisture has evaporated and the butter caramelises. This results in a stronger, sweeter and quite nutty flavour.

Energy 336Kcal/1392kJ; Protein 22g; Carbohydrate 1.2g, of which sugars 0.9g; Fat 27g, of which saturates 10.3g; Cholesterol 92mg; Calcium 9mg; Fibre 0.2g; Sodium 92mg.

LAMB <u>WITH</u> BLACK-EYED BEANS <u>AND</u> PUMPKIN

BLACK-EYED BEANS ARE POPULAR THROUGHOUT AFRICA, AND VERSIONS OF THIS DISH ARE TO BE FOUND FROM MOROCCO TO MALAWI. IT IS IN WEST AFRICA, HOWEVER, THAT THE BEANS ARE MOST WIDELY USED, WHICH EXPLAINS WHY THEY CROP UP IN THE CARIBBEAN, COURTESY OF SLAVES WHO PLANTED THEM TO PROVIDE MEALS WITH A FLAVOUR OF HOME. THE PUMPKIN ADDS A SWEET NOTE.

SERVES FOUR

INGREDIENTS

- 450g/1lb boneless lean lamb or mutton, cubed
- 1 litre/1¾ pints/4 cups chicken or lamb stock or water
- 75g/3oz/scant ½ cup black-eyed beans (peas), soaked for 6 hours, or overnight
- 1 onion, chopped
- 2 garlic cloves, crushed
- 40ml/2½ tbsp tomato purée (paste)
- 7.5ml/1½ tsp dried thyme
- 7.5ml/1½ tsp palm or vegetable oil
- 5ml/1 tsp mixed spice (apple pie spice)
- 2.5ml/½ tsp ground black pepper
- 115g/4oz pumpkin flesh, chopped
- salt and a little hot pepper sauce

1 Put the lamb or mutton in a large pan with the stock or water and bring to the boil. Skim off any foam, then reduce the heat, cover and simmer for 1 hour.

2 Stir in the drained black-eyed beans and continue to cook for about 35 minutes.

VARIATIONS
Mutton is a mature meat with a very good flavour and texture, ideal for stews and casseroles. If mutton is not available, lamb makes a good substitute. Any dried white beans can be used instead of black-eyed beans (peas). If a firmer texture is preferred, cook the pumpkin for about 5 minutes only, until just tender.

3 Add the onion, garlic, tomato purée, thyme, oil, mixed spice, black pepper and salt and hot pepper sauce and cook for a further 15 minutes, until the beans are tender.

4 Add the pumpkin and simmer for 10 minutes, until the pumpkin is very soft or almost mushy. Serve with boiled yam, plantains or sweet potatoes.

Energy 294Kcal/1231kJ; Protein 27.6g; Carbohydrate 15.2g, of which sugars 4.6g; Fat 14.1g, of which saturates 6.1g; Cholesterol 86mg; Calcium 46mg; Fibre 2.6g; Sodium 125mg.

STUFFED LEG ᴼᶠ LAMB, MOROCCAN STYLE

THROUGHOUT NORTH AFRICA, AND IN PARTS OF SPAIN SETTLED BY THE MOORS, THIS IS A FAVOURITE WAY OF COOKING LAMB. THE SPICY RICE STUFFING COMPLEMENTS THE SWEETNESS OF THE MEAT.

SERVES SIX

INGREDIENTS
   1.3–1.6kg/3–3½lb leg of
   lamb, boned
   2 garlic cloves, crushed
   40g/1½oz/3 tbsp butter
   175ml/6fl oz/¾ cup chicken or
   lamb stock
   15ml/1 tbsp cornflour (cornstarch)
   15ml/1 tbsp apricot jam
   salt and ground black pepper
For the stuffing
   1 fresh green chilli, seeded
   2 shallots
   1 garlic clove
   1 bunch of fresh coriander (cilantro)
   sprig of fresh parsley
   25g/1oz/2 tbsp butter
   10ml/2 tsp ground cumin
   2.5ml/½ tsp ground cinnamon
   150g/5oz/¾ cup cooked long
     grain rice
   30ml/2 tbsp pine nuts

1 Preheat the oven to 200°C/400°F/ Gas 6 and then make the stuffing. Place the chilli, shallots, garlic, coriander and parsley in a blender or food processor and process until very finely chopped.

2 Melt the butter in a small frying pan and fry the shallot and herb mixture for 2–3 minutes over a gentle heat to soften the shallots. Add the cumin and cinnamon and stir well.

3 Place the cooked rice in a bowl, add the pine nuts and then stir in the contents of the pan. Season well with salt and pepper. Set aside.

4 Season the meat on both sides with salt and pepper and rub the outside with the crushed garlic and butter. Place the meat, skin side down, on a work surface and spread the stuffing evenly over it. Roll the meat up, secure with a skewer and then tie with cooking string at even intervals.

5 Place in a flameproof roasting pan and roast in the oven for 20 minutes, then reduce the oven temperature to 180°C/ 350°F/Gas 4 and continue to roast for 1½–2 hours, basting occasionally with the juices from the pan.

6 To make the sauce, pour away the excess fat from the roasting pan and then add the chicken stock. Heat gently, stirring all the time, to deglaze the pan.

7 Blend the cornflour with 30ml/ 2 tbsp water and add to the roasting pan together with the apricot jam. Gradually bring to the boil, stirring all the time. Strain the sauce into a serving jug and serve with the stuffed lamb.

Energy 414Kcal/1726kJ; Protein 28.1g; Carbohydrate 13.7g, of which sugars 1.1g; Fat 27.8g, of which saturates 12.9g; Cholesterol 124mg; Calcium 46mg; Fibre 0.9g; Sodium 188mg.

BEEF TAGINE WITH SWEET POTATOES

FEZ IS CREDITED WITH MOROCCO'S FINEST TAGINES. THIS IS A PARTICULARLY GOOD ONE, THE SWEET POTATOES AND WARM SPICES PROVIDING A MELLOW COUNTERPOINT TO THE ROBUST FLAVOUR OF THE BEEF. USE A CASSEROLE WITH A TIGHT-FITTING LID TO MIRROR AS CLOSELY AS POSSIBLE THE EFFECT OF COOKING IN THE TRADITIONAL POT THAT GAVE ITS NAME TO THIS TYPE OF STEW.

SERVES FOUR

INGREDIENTS
  675–900g/1½–2lb braising or
    stewing beef
  30ml/2 tbsp sunflower oil
  good pinch of ground turmeric
  1 large onion, chopped
  1 fresh red or green chilli, seeded
    and finely chopped
  7.5ml/1½ tsp paprika
  good pinch of cayenne pepper
  2.5ml/½ tsp ground cumin
  450g/1lb sweet potatoes
  15ml/1 tbsp chopped fresh parsley
  15ml/1 tbsp chopped fresh
    coriander (cilantro)
  15g/½oz/1 tbsp butter
  salt and ground black pepper

1 Trim the meat and cut into 2cm/¾in cubes. Heat the oil in a flameproof casserole and fry the meat, together with the turmeric and seasoning, over a medium heat for 3–4 minutes, until the meat is evenly browned, stirring frequently.

2 Cover the pan tightly and cook for 15 minutes over a fairly gentle heat, without lifting the lid. Preheat the oven to 180°C/350°F/Gas 4.

3 Add the onion, chilli, paprika, cayenne pepper and cumin to the pan together with just enough water to cover the meat. Cover tightly and cook in the oven for 1–1½ hours, until the meat is very tender, checking occasionally and adding a little extra water, if necessary, to keep the stew fairly moist.

4 Meanwhile, peel the sweet potatoes and slice them straight into a bowl of salted water to avoid discolouring. Transfer to a pan, bring to the boil, simmer for 2–3 minutes. Drain.

5 Stir the chopped herbs into the meat, adding a little extra water if the stew appears dry. Arrange the potato slices over the meat and dot with the butter. Cover and cook in the oven for a further 10 minutes, until the potatoes feel very tender. Increase the oven temperature to 200°C/400°F/Gas 6 or preheat the grill (broiler) to its hottest setting.

6 Remove the lid of the casserole and cook in the oven or under the grill for a further 5–10 minutes, until the potatoes are golden. Serve at once.

VARIATIONS
You can use lean lamb instead of beef. Use swede (rutabaga) in place of the sweet potatoes.

Energy 434Kcal/1819kJ; Protein 39.1g; Carbohydrate 28.9g, of which sugars 10g; Fat 18.8g, of which saturates 6.8g; Cholesterol 114mg; Calcium 66mg; Fibre 3.9g; Sodium 180mg.

EAST AFRICAN ROAST CHICKEN

RUBBING THE SKIN ON THE CHICKEN WITH A SPICY HERB BUTTER AND THEN MARINATING IT OVERNIGHT GIVES IT A WONDERFUL FLAVOUR. BASTE IT FREQUENTLY WHILE IT COOKS.

SERVES SIX

INGREDIENTS

1.8–2kg/4–4½lb chicken
30ml/2 tbsp softened butter, plus
   extra for basting
3 garlic cloves, crushed
5ml/1 tsp ground black pepper
5ml/1 tsp ground turmeric
2.5ml/½ tsp ground cumin
5ml/1 tsp dried thyme
15ml/1 tbsp finely chopped fresh
   coriander (cilantro)
60ml/4 tbsp thick coconut milk
60ml/4 tbsp medium-dry sherry
5ml/1 tsp tomato purée (paste)
salt and chilli powder

1 Remove and discard the giblets from the chicken, if necessary, rinse out the cavity and pat the skin dry. Put the butter and all the remaining ingredients in a bowl and mix together well to form a thick paste.

2 Ease the skin of the chicken away from the flesh and push in some of the herb and butter mixture. Rub more of the mixture over the skin, legs and wings of the chicken.

3 Place the chicken in a roasting pan, cover loosely with foil and marinate overnight in the fridge.

VARIATION
Use ground coriander instead of ground cumin or dried thyme.

4 Preheat the oven to 190°C/375°F/ Gas 5. Cover the chicken with clean foil and roast for 1 hour, then turn the chicken over and baste with the pan juices. Cover again with foil and roast for a further 30 minutes.

5 Remove the foil and place the chicken breast side up. Rub with a little extra butter and roast for a further 10–15 minutes, until the meat juices run clear and the skin is golden brown. Serve with a rice dish or a salad.

YASSA CHICKEN

OFTEN DESCRIBED AS THE NATIONAL DISH OF SENEGAL, YASSA CAN BE MADE WITH CHICKEN, TURKEY OR FISH. THE LEMON JUICE MARINADE GIVES THE SAUCE ITS TYPICALLY TANGY TASTE.

SERVES FOUR

INGREDIENTS

150ml/¼ pint/⅔ cup lemon juice
60ml/4 tbsp malt vinegar
3 onions, sliced
60ml/4 tbsp groundnut (peanut) or
   vegetable oil
1kg/2¼lb chicken pieces
1 fresh thyme sprig
1 fresh green chilli, seeded and
   finely chopped
2 bay leaves
450ml/¾ pint/scant 2 cups
   chicken stock

VARIATION
For a less tangy flavour, you can add less lemon juice, although it does mellow after cooking.

1 Mix the lemon juice, vinegar, onions and 30ml/2 tbsp of the oil together, place the chicken pieces in a dish and pour over the lemon mixture. Cover and leave in a cool place for 3 hours.

2 Heat the remaining oil in a large pan and fry the chicken pieces for 4–5 minutes, until browned.

3 Add the marinated onions to the chicken. Fry for 3 minutes, then add the marinade, thyme, chilli, bay leaves and half the stock.

4 Reduce the heat, cover the pan and simmer for about 35 minutes, until the chicken is cooked, add more stock as the sauce evaporates. Serve hot.

TOP Energy 439Kcal/1824kJ; Protein 43.3g; Carbohydrate 1.2g, of which sugars 1.2g; Fat 27.9g, of which saturates 10.7g; Cholesterol 206mg; Calcium 23mg; Fibre 0g; Sodium 211mg.
BOTTOM Energy 462Kcal/1918kJ; Protein 37.4g; Carbohydrate 8.9g, of which sugars 6.3g; Fat 31g, of which saturates 8g; Cholesterol 163mg; Calcium 43mg; Fibre 1.6g; Sodium 141mg.

MARRAKESH ROAST CHICKEN

MOROCCANS INVENTED THE SPICE RUB LONG BEFORE IT BECAME A TRENDY DELI ITEM. FOR THIS TRADITIONAL DISH, A PASTE MADE FROM SHALLOTS, GARLIC, FRESH HERBS AND SPICES IS RUBBED INTO THE CHICKEN SKIN A FEW HOURS BEFORE ROASTING, SO THE FLAVOUR PERMEATES THE FLESH.

SERVES FOUR TO SIX

INGREDIENTS
  1.8–2kg/4–4½lb chicken
  2 small shallots
  1 garlic clove
  1 fresh parsley sprig
  1 fresh coriander (cilantro) sprig
  5ml/1 tsp salt
  7.5ml/1½ tsp paprika
  pinch of cayenne pepper
  5–7.5ml/1–1½ tsp ground cumin
  about 40g/1½oz/3 tbsp butter,
    at room temperature
  ½–1 lemon (optional)
  sprigs of fresh parsley or coriander
    (cilantro), to garnish

VARIATION
If you are unable to buy shallots, use one small onion instead.

1 Remove and discard the chicken giblets, if necessary, and rinse out the cavity with cold running water. Unless cooking it whole, cut the chicken in half or into quarters using poultry shears or a sharp knife.

2 Place the shallots, garlic, herbs, salt and spices in a blender or food processor and process until the shallots are finely chopped. Add the butter and process to make a smooth paste.

3 Thoroughly rub the paste over the skin of the chicken and then allow it to stand in a cool place for 1–2 hours.

4 Preheat the oven to 200°C/400°F/ Gas 6 and place the chicken in a roasting pan. If using, quarter the lemon and place one or two quarters around the chicken pieces (or in the body cavity if the chicken is whole) and squeeze a little juice over the skin.

5 Roast the chicken in the oven for 1–1¼ hours (2–2¼ hours for a whole bird), until the chicken is cooked through and the meat juices run clear. Baste occasionally during cooking with the juices in the roasting pan. If the skin browns too quickly, cover the chicken loosely with foil or greaseproof (waxed) paper.

6 Allow the chicken to stand for 5–10 minutes, covered in foil, before serving, and then serve garnished with sprigs of fresh parsley or coriander.

Energy 559Kcal/2323kJ; Protein 54.1g; Carbohydrate 0.2g, of which sugars 0.2g; Fat 37.9g, of which saturates 15.3g; Cholesterol 265mg; Calcium 25mg; Fibre 0.1g; Sodium 759mg.

CHICKEN AND PRESERVED LEMON TAGINE

MOROCCAN TAGINES ARE SUBTLY FLAVOURED STEWS WHICH ARE COOKED IN THE CONICAL-LIDDED DISHES FROM WHICH THEY GET THEIR NAME. THIS IS THE MOST FAMOUS TAGINE RECIPE, IN WHICH THE PRESERVED LEMON'S MELLOW FLAVOUR CONTRASTS WITH THE EARTHINESS OF THE OLIVES.

SERVES FOUR

INGREDIENTS
    30ml/2 tbsp olive oil
    1 Spanish onion, chopped
    3 garlic cloves
    1cm/½in fresh root ginger, peeled
      and grated, or 2.5ml/½ tsp
      ground ginger
    2.5–5ml/½–1 tsp ground cinnamon
    pinch of saffron threads
    4 chicken quarters, preferably
      breasts, halved if liked
    750ml/1¼ pints/3 cups
      chicken stock
    30ml/2 tbsp chopped fresh
      coriander (cilantro)
    30ml/2 tbsp chopped fresh parsley
    1 preserved lemon
    115g/4oz/⅔ cup Moroccan tan olives
    salt and ground black pepper
    lemon wedges and fresh coriander
      (cilantro) sprigs, to garnish

1 Heat the oil in a large flameproof casserole and fry the onion for 6–8 minutes over a moderate heat until lightly golden, stirring occasionally.

2 Meanwhile, crush the garlic and blend with the ginger, cinnamon, saffron and a little salt and pepper. Stir into the pan and fry for 1 minute.

3 Add the chicken quarters to the pan, in batches if necessary, and fry over a medium heat for 2–3 minutes, until lightly browned.

4 Add the stock, chopped coriander and parsley, bring to the boil and then cover and simmer very gently for 45 minutes, until the chicken is tender.

5 Rinse the preserved lemon, discard the flesh and cut the peel into small pieces. Stir into the pan with the olives and simmer for a further 15 minutes, until the chicken is very tender.

6 Transfer the chicken to a plate and keep warm. Bring the sauce to the boil and bubble for 3–4 minutes, until reduced and fairly thick.

7 Pour the sauce over the chicken and serve, garnished with lemon wedges and coriander sprigs.

Energy 474Kcal/1967kJ; Protein 36.3g; Carbohydrate 5.3g, of which sugars 3.8g; Fat 34.3g, of which saturates 8.1g; Cholesterol 209mg; Calcium 83mg; Fibre 2.6g; Sodium 807mg.

JOLOFF CHICKEN AND RICE

FEW VISITORS TO WEST AFRICA FAIL TO TRY THIS FESTIVE CHICKEN AND RICE DISH. IT IS RICHLY FLAVOURED WITH TOMATOES AND CAN BE MADE WITH CHICKEN, BEEF OR JUST WITH VEGETABLES.

SERVES FOUR

INGREDIENTS
1kg/2¼lb chicken, cut into
  4–6 pieces
2 garlic cloves, crushed
5ml/1 tsp dried thyme
30ml/2 tbsp palm or vegetable oil
400g/14oz can chopped tomatoes
15ml/1 tbsp tomato purée (paste)
1 onion, chopped
450ml/¾ pint/scant 2 cups
  chicken stock
30ml/2 tbsp dried shrimps, ground
1 fresh green chilli, seeded and
  finely chopped
350g/12oz/1¾ cups long grain
  rice, washed

1 Rub the chicken with the garlic and thyme and set aside.

2 Heat the oil in a pan and brown the chicken pieces. Add the tomatoes, tomato purée and onion. Cook over a medium-high heat for about 5 minutes, stirring occasionally at first then more frequently as it thickens.

3 Add the stock and stir well. Bring to the boil, then reduce the heat, cover and simmer for 40 minutes. Add the shrimps and chilli. Cook for 5 minutes.

4 Put the rice in a pan. Scoop 300ml/½ pint/1¼ cups of tomato stock from the chicken into a measuring jug (cup), top up with water to 450ml/¾ pint/scant 2 cups and add to the rice. Cook for 10 minutes to partly absorb the liquid.

5 Place a piece of foil on top of the rice, cover and cook over a low heat for 10 minutes, adding a little more water if necessary. Transfer the chicken pieces to a serving plate. Simmer the sauce until reduced by half. Pour over the chicken and serve with the rice.

Energy 719Kcal/2998kJ; Protein 44.1g; Carbohydrate 76.3g, of which sugars 5.4g; Fat 25.9g, of which saturates 7.4g; Cholesterol 163mg; Calcium 54mg; Fibre 1.3g; Sodium 187mg.

KUKU

THIS DELICIOUS TANGY CHICKEN STEW COMES FROM KENYA. THE SAUCE IS THICKENED WITH MASHED MUNG BEANS, AND FLAVOURED WITH CHILLI AND COCONUT MILK.

SERVES FOUR TO SIX

INGREDIENTS
    6 chicken thighs or pieces
    2.5–4ml/½–¾ tsp ground ginger
    50g/2oz dried mung beans
    60ml/4 tbsp corn oil
    2 onions, finely chopped
    2 garlic cloves, crushed
    5 tomatoes, skinned and chopped
    1 fresh green chilli, seeded and
        finely chopped
    30ml/2 tbsp lemon juice
    300ml/½ pint/1¼ cups coconut milk
    300ml/½ pint/1¼ cups water
    15ml/1 tbsp chopped fresh
        coriander (cilantro)
    salt and ground black pepper

1 Season the chicken pieces with the ginger and a little salt and pepper and set aside in a cool place. Boil the mung beans in plenty of water for 35 minutes until soft. Drain and mash.

2 Heat the oil in a large pan over a medium heat and fry the chicken pieces, in batches if necessary, until evenly browned. Transfer to a plate and set aside. Reserve the juices in the pan.

3 In the same pan, fry the onions and garlic for 5 minutes, then add the chopped tomatoes and green chilli and cook for a further 1–2 minutes, stirring all the time. Add the mashed mung beans and lemon juice.

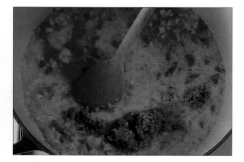

4 Pour the coconut milk in to the pan. Simmer for 5 minutes, then add the chicken pieces and a little water if the sauce is too thick. Stir in the chopped coriander and simmer for about 35 minutes, until the chicken is cooked through. Serve with a green vegetable and rice or chapatis.

Energy 257Kcal/1089kJ; Protein 41.1g; Carbohydrate 18.7g, of which sugars 11.3g; Fat 2.6g, of which saturates 0.8g; Cholesterol 105mg; Calcium 81mg; Fibre 3.7g; Sodium 188mg.

BISTILLA

One of the most elaborate dishes in Moroccan cuisine, bistilla often forms the centrepiece at a feast or banquet. It is traditionally made using pigeon, cooked with spices and layered with the wafer-thin pastry known as ouarka. The pie is then cooked over hot coals. This is a simplified version, using filo pastry, which is much easier to handle than ouarka. The dusting of cinnamon and icing sugar on top of the pie is a typical North African refinement, also used on briouates.

SERVES FOUR

INGREDIENTS
    30ml/2 tbsp sunflower oil, plus extra
       for brushing
    25g/1oz/2 tbsp butter
    3 chicken quarters, preferably breasts
    1½ Spanish onions, grated or very
       finely chopped
    good pinch of ground ginger
    good pinch of saffron threads
    10ml/2 tsp ground cinnamon, plus
       extra for dusting
    40g/1½oz/4 tbsp flaked
       (sliced) almonds
    1 large bunch of fresh coriander
       (cilantro), finely chopped
    1 large bunch of fresh parsley,
       finely chopped
    3 eggs, beaten
    about 175g/6oz filo pastry sheets
    5–10ml/1–2 tsp icing (confectioners')
       sugar (optional), plus extra
       for dusting
    salt and ground black pepper

1 Heat the oil and butter in a large flameproof casserole or pan until the butter is melted. Add the chicken pieces and brown for about 4 minutes.

2 Add the onions, ginger, saffron, 2.5ml/½ tsp of the cinnamon and enough water (about 300ml/½ pint/1¼ cups) so that the chicken braises, rather than boils. Season well with salt and pepper.

3 Bring to the boil and then cover and simmer very gently for 45–55 minutes, until the chicken is tender and completely cooked. Meanwhile, dry-fry the almonds in a separate small pan until golden and then set aside.

4 Transfer the chicken to a plate and, when cool enough to handle, remove and discard the skin and bones and cut the flesh into pieces.

5 Stir the chopped coriander and parsley into the pan and simmer the sauce until well reduced and thick. Add the beaten eggs and cook over a very gentle heat until the eggs are lightly scrambled.

6 Preheat the oven to 180°C/350°F/ Gas 4. Oil a shallow round ovenproof dish, about 25cm/10in in diameter.

7 Place one or two sheets of filo pastry in a single layer over the bottom of the dish (it will depend on the size of your filo pastry sheets), so that it is completely covered and the edges of the pastry sheets hang over the sides. Brush lightly with oil and make two more layers of filo, brushing with oil between the layers.

8 Place the chicken on the pastry and then spoon the egg and herb mixture on top and spread evenly.

9 Place a single layer of filo pastry on top of the filling (you may need to use more than one sheet of filo pastry).

10 Scatter the almonds over the layer of filo pastry. Sprinkle with some of the remaining cinnamon and the icing sugar, if using.

11 Fold the edges of the filo over the almonds and then make four further layers of filo (using one or two sheets of filo per layer, depending on size), brushing each layer with a little oil. Tuck the filo edges under the pie (as if you were making a bed!) and brush the top layer with oil.

12 Bake in the oven for 40–45 minutes, until golden. Dust the top with icing sugar and use the extra cinnamon to make criss-cross or diagonal lines. Serve immediately.

VARIATIONS
Use standard large onions instead of Spanish onions. Use flaked hazelnuts or whole pine nuts instead of flaked almonds.

Energy 653Kcal/2720kJ; Protein 39.2g; Carbohydrate 33.6g, of which sugars 7.1g; Fat 41.3g, of which saturates 11g; Cholesterol 321mg; Calcium 176mg; Fibre 4.4g; Sodium 224mg.

VEGETARIAN DISHES, SALADS AND ACCOMPANIMENTS

The concept of vegetarian dishes and accompaniments is not as clearly defined in Africa as it is in Europe and America, however, there are some exciting dishes to be had. Rice is served at many meals, either plain or with extra ingredients, as in the Tanzanian Vegetable Rice or West African Joloff. Breads are present at almost every meal, while salads are intriguing, often introducing elements that are relatively unknown outside the country of origin.

CLASSIC CASABLANCAN COUSCOUS WITH ROASTED SUMMER VEGETABLES

THIS DISH IS BASED ON THE TRADITION THAT A STEW SERVED WITH COUSCOUS SHOULD INCLUDE SEVEN VEGETABLES. THE NUMBER SEVEN IS SAID TO BRING GOOD LUCK, AND ANY SUITABLE COMBINATION OF VEGETABLES CAN BE USED, AS LONG AS THE TOTAL ADDS UP TO THE MAGIC NUMBER. TO ADD A FLICKER OF FIRE TO THIS DISH, SERVE IT WITH A SPOONFUL OF HARISSA. TO COOL THE PALATE, OFFER A BOWL OF THICK AND CREAMY YOGURT.

SERVES SIX

INGREDIENTS

3 red onions, peeled and quartered
2–3 courgettes (zucchini), halved
  lengthways and cut across into
  2–3 pieces
2–3 red, green or yellow (bell)
  peppers, seeded and quartered
2 aubergines (eggplants), cut into
  6–8 long segments
2–3 leeks, trimmed and cut into
  long strips
2–3 sweet potatoes, peeled,
  halved lengthways and cut
  into long strips
4–6 tomatoes, quartered
6 garlic cloves, crushed
25g/1oz fresh root ginger, sliced
a few large fresh rosemary sprigs
about 150ml/¼ pint/⅔ cup olive oil
10ml/2 tsp clear honey
salt and ground black pepper
natural (plain) yogurt or harissa and
  bread, to serve
For the couscous
  500g/1¼lb/3 cups couscous
  5ml/1 tsp salt
  600ml/1 pint/2½ cups warm water
  45ml/3 tbsp sunflower oil
  about 25g/1oz/2 tbsp butter, diced

1 Preheat the oven to 200°C/400°F/ Gas 6. Arrange all the vegetables in a roasting pan. Tuck the garlic, ginger and rosemary around the vegetables.

2 Pour lots of olive oil over the vegetables, drizzle with the honey, add salt and pepper, and then roast for about 1½ hours until they are extremely tender and slightly caramelized. The cooking time will depend on the size of the vegetable pieces. Turn them in the oil occasionally.

3 When the vegetables are nearly ready, put the couscous in a bowl. Stir the salt into the water, then pour it over the couscous, stirring to make sure it is absorbed evenly. Leave to stand for 10 minutes to plump up then, using your fingers, rub the sunflower oil into the grains to air them and break up any lumps. Tip the couscous into an ovenproof dish, arrange the butter over the top, cover with foil and heat in the oven for about 20 minutes.

4 To serve, use your fingers to work the melted butter into the grains of couscous and fluff it up, then pile it on a large dish and shape into a mound with a little pit at the top. Spoon some vegetables into the pit and arrange the rest around the dish. Pour the oil from the pan over the couscous or serve separately. Serve immediately with yogurt, or harissa if you prefer, and bread for mopping up the juices.

Energy 561Kcal/2340kJ; Protein 10.4g; Carbohydrate 78.8g, of which sugars 18.7g; Fat 24.6g, of which saturates 3.5g; Cholesterol 0mg; Calcium 101mg; Fibre 7.3g; Sodium 51mg.

TAGINE OF ARTICHOKE HEARTS, POTATOES, PEAS AND SAFFRON

ARTICHOKES ARE A DELICACY EATEN IN NORTH AFRICA, AND WHEN THE SEASON STARTS, COOKS COMPETE FOR THE PICK OF THE CROP. IN SOME MARKETS IT IS POSSIBLE TO BUY JUST THE ARTICHOKE HEARTS, WHICH SAVES THE SOMEWHAT TEDIOUS TASK OF PREPARATION AT HOME. IF YOU DO NEED TO DO THIS YOURSELF, FIRST REMOVE THE OUTER LEAVES, THEN CUT OFF THE STEMS AND SCOOP OUT THE CHOKE AND THE HAIRY BITS WITH A TEASPOON.

SERVES FOUR TO SIX

INGREDIENTS
  6 fresh globe artichoke hearts
  juice of 1 lemon
  30–45ml/2–3 tbsp olive oil
  1 onion, chopped
  675g/1½lb potatoes, peeled
    and quartered
  small bunch of fresh flat leaf
    parsley, chopped
  small bunch of fresh coriander
    (cilantro), chopped
  small bunch of fresh mint, chopped
  pinch of saffron threads
  5ml/1 tsp ground turmeric
  about 350ml/12fl oz/1½ cups
    vegetable stock
  finely chopped rind of
    ½ preserved lemon
  250g/9oz/2¼ cups shelled peas
  salt and ground black pepper
  couscous or bread, to serve

COOK'S TIP
When preparing artichokes, once cut, the flesh of artichokes will blacken. To prevent this from happening, put the artichokes into acidulated water – you can use lemon juice or white wine vinegar.

1 Poach the artichoke hearts very gently in plenty of simmering water with half the lemon juice, for 10–15 minutes, until tender. Drain and refresh under cold water, then drain again.

2 Heat the olive oil in a tagine or heavy pan. Add the onion and cook over a low heat for about 15 minutes, until softened but not browned. Add the potatoes, most of the chopped parsley, the chopped coriander and mint, the remaining lemon juice, and the saffron and turmeric to the pan.

3 Pour in the stock, bring to the boil, then reduce the heat. Cover the pan and cook for about 15 minutes, until the potatoes are almost tender.

4 Stir the preserved lemon, artichoke hearts and peas into the stew, and cook, uncovered, for a further 10 minutes. Season to taste, sprinkle with the remaining parsley, and serve with couscous or chunks of fresh bread.

Energy 260Kcal/1089kJ; Protein 8.6g; Carbohydrate 42g, of which sugars 10.6g; Fat 7.5g, of which saturates 1.2g; Cholesterol 0mg; Calcium 96mg; Fibre 7.9g; Sodium 47mg.

TAGINE OF YAM, CARROTS AND PRUNES

THE YAMS IN THIS MOROCCAN DISH REVEAL A WEST AFRICAN INFLUENCE. IT COMES FROM THE ATLAS MOUNTAINS, WHERE THE TEMPERATURE OFTEN DROPS TO BELOW ZERO IN WINTER, AND WARMING STEWS ARE VERY WELCOME. THIS IS QUITE A SWEET-TASTING DISH, THANKS TO THE CARAMELIZED VEGETABLES AND THE PRUNES. SERVE IT WITH COUSCOUS AND A GREEN SALAD THAT INCLUDES SOME BITTER LEAVES, PREFERABLY WITH A SHARP LEMON AND OIL DRESSING.

SERVES FOUR TO SIX

INGREDIENTS
    45ml/3 tbsp olive oil
    a little butter
    25–30 button (pearl) onions,
      blanched and peeled
    900g/2lb yam or sweet potatoes,
      peeled and cut into bitesize chunks
    2–3 carrots, cut into bitesize chunks
    150g/5oz/generous ½ cup ready-to-
      eat pitted prunes
    5ml/1 tsp ground cinnamon
    2.5ml/½ tsp ground ginger
    10ml/2 tsp clear honey
    450ml/¾ pint/scant 2 cups
      vegetable stock
    small bunch of fresh coriander
      (cilantro), finely chopped
    small bunch of fresh mint,
      finely chopped
    salt and ground black pepper

COOK'S TIP
Yams have a brown skin and cream-coloured flesh; sweet potatoes have dark red or orange skin and orange flesh. Buy firm specimens that do not "give".

1 Preheat the oven to 200°C/400°F/ Gas 6. Heat the olive oil in a flameproof casserole with the butter and stir in the onions. Cook for about 5 minutes until the onions are tender, then remove half of the onions from the pan and set aside.

2 Add the yam or sweet potatoes and carrots to the pan and cook until lightly browned. Stir in the prunes with the cinnamon, ginger and honey, then pour in the stock. Season well, cover the casserole and transfer to the oven for about 45 minutes.

3 Stir in the reserved onions and bake for a further 10 minutes. Gently stir in the chopped coriander and mint, and serve the tagine immediately.

Energy 454Kcal/1922kJ; Protein 6.2g; Carbohydrate 91.8g, of which sugars 27.1g; Fat 9.5g, of which saturates 1.5g; Cholesterol 0mg; Calcium 111mg; Fibre 7.9g; Sodium 32mg.

BUTTER BEAN, TOMATO AND OLIVE TAGINE

VEGETARIANS SOMETIMES STRUGGLE TO FIND SOMETHING HOT AND SUBSTANTIAL TO EAT WHEN TRAVELLING IN AFRICA, AS EVEN VEGETABLE STEWS ARE OFTEN MADE WITH MEAT STOCK. THIS TAGINE TAKES ITS MOISTURE FROM TOMATOES AND OLIVE OIL, HOWEVER, SO FITS THE BILL PERFECTLY. IT IS HEARTY ENOUGH TO BE SERVED ON ITS OWN, WITH FRESH, CRUSTY BREAD AND PERHAPS A SALAD. IF YOU ARE SERVING IT TO NON-VEGETARIANS, ADD SOME SLICED CHORIZO.

SERVES FOUR

INGREDIENTS

115g/4oz/⅔ cup butter (lima) beans, soaked overnight
30–45ml/2–3 tbsp olive oil
1 onion, chopped
2–3 garlic cloves, crushed
25g/1oz fresh root ginger, peeled and finely chopped
pinch of saffron threads
16 cherry tomatoes
generous pinch of granulated sugar
handful of fleshy black olives, pitted
5ml/1 tsp ground cinnamon
5ml/1 tsp paprika
small bunch of fresh flat leaf parsley
salt and ground black pepper

1 Rinse the beans and place them in a large pan with plenty of water. Bring to the boil and boil for about 10 minutes, and then reduce the heat and simmer gently for 1–1½ hours until tender. Drain the beans and refresh under cold running water, then drain again.

COOK'S TIP
If you are in a hurry, you could use two 400g/14oz cans of butter (lima) beans for this tagine. Make sure you rinse the them well before adding, as canned beans tend to be salty.

2 Heat the olive oil in a heavy pan. Add the onion, garlic and ginger, and cook for about 10 minutes, until softened but not browned. Stir in the saffron threads, followed by the cherry tomatoes and a sprinkling of sugar.

3 As the tomatoes begin to soften, stir in the butter beans. When the tomatoes have heated through, stir in the olives, ground cinnamon and paprika. Season to taste and sprinkle over the chopped parsley. Serve immediately.

Energy 146Kcal/615kJ; Protein 7.4g; Carbohydrate 16.2g, of which sugars 3.8g; Fat 6.3g, of which saturates 0.9g; Cholesterol 0mg; Calcium 62mg; Fibre 6g; Sodium 16mg.

OKRA AND TOMATO TAGINE

ALTHOUGH THIS VEGETABLE STEW IS A NORTH AFRICAN SPECIALITY, SIMILAR DISHES EXIST THROUGHOUT THE MIDDLE EAST. OKRA IS PARTICULARLY POPULAR IN EGYPT, WHERE IT IS CULTIVATED COMMERCIALLY ON A GRAND SCALE. WHEN CUT BEFORE BEING COOKED, AS IN THIS RECIPE, THE PODS OOZE A GLUE-LIKE SUBSTANCE WHICH GIVES THE DISH A DISTINCTIVE TEXTURE.

SERVES FOUR

INGREDIENTS
- 350g/12oz okra
- 5–6 tomatoes
- 2 small onions
- 2 garlic cloves, crushed
- 1 fresh green chilli, seeded
- 5ml/1 tsp paprika
- small handful of fresh
  coriander (cilantro)
- 30ml/2 tbsp sunflower oil
- juice of 1 lemon

1 Trim the okra and then cut it into 1cm/½in lengths. Skin and seed the tomatoes and roughly chop the flesh.

2 Roughly chop one of the onions and place it in a blender or food processor with the garlic, chilli, paprika, coriander and 60ml/4 tbsp water. Process to make a paste.

3 Thinly slice the second onion and fry it in the oil in a pan for 5–6 minutes, until golden brown. Transfer to a plate and set aside. Reduce the heat and pour the onion and coriander paste into the pan. Cook for 1–2 minutes, stirring frequently.

4 Add the okra, tomatoes, lemon juice and about 120ml/4fl oz/½ cup water. Stir well to mix, cover tightly and simmer over a low heat for about 15 minutes, until the okra is tender. Transfer to a serving dish, sprinkle with the fried onion rings and serve.

VARIATION
Use 3–4 shallots instead of onions.

Energy 113Kcal/471kJ; Protein 4.1g; Carbohydrate 9.2g, of which sugars 8g; Fat 7g, of which saturates 1.1g; Cholesterol 0mg; Calcium 181mg; Fibre 5.8g; Sodium 23mg.

CHICKPEA TAGINE

THE PRESERVED LEMON IN THIS RECIPE TELLS YOU THAT IT COMES FROM NORTH AFRICA, PROBABLY MOROCCO, WHERE THE DISTINCTIVE YELLOW GLOBES IN GLASS JARS GLIMMER LIKE MINIATURE SUNS IN THE MARKETS. THE FLAVOUR OF PRESERVED — OR PICKLED — LEMON IS WONDERFUL. SLIGHTLY SALTY, LESS TART THAN THE FRESH FRUIT, IT ADDS A REAL ZING TO THE BLANDNESS OF THE CHICKPEAS.

SERVES FOUR

INGREDIENTS
    150g/5oz/¾ cup chickpeas, soaked
        overnight, or 2 x 400g/14oz cans
        chickpeas, rinsed and drained
    30ml/2 tbsp sunflower oil
    1 large onion, chopped
    1 garlic clove, crushed (optional)
    400g/14oz can chopped tomatoes
    5ml/1 tsp ground cumin
    350ml/12fl oz/1½ cups
        vegetable stock
    ¼ preserved lemon
    30ml/2 tbsp chopped fresh
        coriander (cilantro)

1 If using dried chickpeas, cook them in plenty of boiling water for 1–1½ hours until tender. Drain well.

2 Place the chickpeas in a bowl of cold water and rub them between your fingers to remove the skins.

3 Heat the oil in a pan or flameproof casserole and fry the onion and garlic, if using, for 8–10 minutes, until golden.

4 Add the chickpeas, tomatoes, cumin and stock and stir well. Bring to the boil and simmer, uncovered, for 30–40 minutes, until the chickpeas are very soft and most of the liquid has evaporated.

5 Rinse the preserved lemon and cut away the flesh and pith. Cut the peel into slivers and stir it into the chickpeas together with the chopped coriander. Serve immediately with Moroccan bread.

Energy 207Kcal/871kJ; Protein 9.7g; Carbohydrate 26.4g, of which sugars 7.1g; Fat 7.8g, of which saturates 0.9g; Cholesterol 0mg; Calcium 87mg; Fibre 5.6g; Sodium 56mg.

SUMMER VEGETABLE KEBABS
WITH HARISSA AND YOGURT DIP

THERE'S NOTHING NEW ABOUT THREADING VEGETABLE CHUNKS ON SKEWERS, BUT THIS METHOD OF TOSSING THEM IN A SPICY OIL AND LEMON JUICE MARINADE MAKES ALL THE DIFFERENCE. SERVE THEM WITH THE HOT AND CREAMY DIP AND YOU'LL HAVE VEGETARIAN GUESTS EATING OUT OF YOUR HANDS — OR THEIRS. THE KEBABS CAN ALSO BE COOKED ON THE BARBECUE.

SERVES FOUR

INGREDIENTS
    2 aubergines (eggplants), part peeled
      and cut into chunks
    2 courgettes (zucchini), cut
      into chunks
    2–3 red or green (bell) peppers,
      seeded and cut into chunks
    12–16 cherry tomatoes
    4 small red onions, quartered
    60ml/4 tbsp olive oil
    juice of ½ lemon
    1 garlic clove, crushed
    5ml/1 tsp ground coriander
    5ml/1 tsp ground cinnamon
    10ml/2 tsp clear honey
    5ml/1 tsp salt
For the harissa and yogurt dip
    450g/1lb/2 cups Greek (US strained
      plain) yogurt
    30–60ml/2–4 tbsp harissa
    small bunch of fresh coriander
      (cilantro), finely chopped
    small bunch of mint, finely chopped
    salt and ground black pepper

1 Preheat the grill (broiler) on the hottest setting. Put all the vegetables in a bowl. Mix together the olive oil, lemon juice, garlic, ground coriander, cinnamon, honey and salt and pour the mixture over the vegetables.

2 Using your hands, turn the vegetables gently in the marinade, then thread them on to metal skewers. Cook the kebabs under the grill, turning them occasionally, until the vegetables are nicely browned all over.

3 To make the dip, put
bowl and beat in the ha
as fiery in taste as you li
more harissa. Add most
coriander and mint, rese
garnish, and season well
pepper. While they are s
vegetables off the skewe
into the yogurt dip befor
Garnish with the reserve

COOK'S TIP
Make sure you cut the au
courgettes and peppers ir
size chunks, so they will
same rate.

Energy 274Kcal/1144kJ; Protein 11.1g; Carbohydrate 28.8g, of which sugars 26.2g; Fat 13.7g, of which saturates 2.5g; Cholesterol 1mg; Calcium 303mg; Fibre 5.

COUS WITH DRIED FRUIT, NUTS
NNAMON

*, THIS DISH OF COUSCOUS WITH DATES, RAISINS AND NUTS FREQUENTLY FORMS PART OF
N MEAL. THE DISH IS OFTEN SERVED AS A COURSE ON ITS OWN, JUST BEFORE THE
LSO TASTES GOOD WITH A SPICY TAGINE, OR AS A SIDE DISH WITH ROASTED OR GRILLED
LTRY. THE SUGAR AND CINNAMON MIXTURE IS TRADITIONALLY SPRINKLED IN STRIPES.*

cups couscous
2½ cups warm water

n threads
unflower oil
ive oil
or smen
up dried apricots,
rs
dried dates, chopped
ous ½ cup
ns
up blanched almonds,
rs
pistachio nuts
und cinnamon
aster (superfine) sugar

1 Preheat the oven to 180°C/350°F/
Gas 4. Put the couscous in a bowl. Mix
together the water, salt and saffron and
pour it over the couscous, stirring.
Leave to stand for 10 minutes. Add the
sunflower oil and, using your fingers,
rub it through the grains. Set aside.

2 In a heavy pan, heat the olive oil and
butter or smen and stir in the apricots,
dates, raisins, most of the almonds
(reserve some for garnish) and
pistachio nuts.

3 Cook until the raisins plump up, then
tip the nuts and fruit into the couscous
and toss together to mix. Tip the
couscous into an ovenproof dish and
cover with foil. Place in the oven for
about 20 minutes, until heated through.

4 Toast the reserved slivered almonds.
Pile the hot couscous in a mound on a
large serving dish and sprinkle with the
cinnamon and sugar – these are usually
sprinkled in stripes down the mound.
Scatter the toasted almonds over the
top and serve hot.

Protein 11.9g; Carbohydrate 71.5g, of which sugars 27.9g; Fat 27.7g, of which saturates 3g; Cholesterol 0mg; Calcium 94mg; Fibre 3.3g; Sodium 79mg.

EGUSI SPINACH AND EGG

THIS IS A SUPERBLY BALANCED DISH FOR THOSE WHO DON'T EAT MEAT. EGUSI, OR GROUND MELON SEED, IS WIDELY USED IN WEST AFRICAN COOKING AND ADDS A CREAMY TEXTURE AND A NUTTY FLAVOUR TO MANY RECIPES. IT IS ESPECIALLY GOOD WITH FRESH SPINACH AND TOMATOES.

SERVES FOUR

INGREDIENTS
    900g/2lb fresh spinach
    115g/4oz egusi
    90ml/6 tbsp groundnut (peanut)
        or vegetable oil
    4 tomatoes, skinned and chopped
    1 onion, chopped
    2 garlic cloves, crushed
    1 slice of fresh root ginger, peeled
        and finely chopped
    150ml/¼ pint/⅔ cup vegetable stock
    1 fresh red chilli, seeded and
        finely chopped
    6 eggs
    salt

1 Roll the spinach into bundles and cut into strips. Place in a bowl.

2 Cover with boiling water, then drain through a sieve. Press with your fingers to remove excess water. Set aside.

3 Place the egusi in a bowl and gradually add enough water to form a paste, stirring all the time. Set aside.

4 Heat the oil in a pan, add the tomatoes, onion, garlic and ginger and fry over a medium heat for about 10 minutes, stirring frequently.

5 Add the egusi paste, stock, chilli and salt, cook for 10 minutes, then add the spinach and stir it into the sauce. Cook for 15 minutes, uncovered, stirring frequently.

6 Meanwhile hard-boil the eggs, and then stand them in cold water for a few minutes to cool. Shell the eggs and then cut them in half. Arrange the eggs in a shallow serving dish and pour the egusi spinach over the top. Serve hot.

VARIATION
Instead of using boiled eggs, you could make an omelette flavoured with chopped herbs and garlic. Serve it either whole, or sliced, with the egusi sauce. If you can't find egusi, use ground almonds as a substitute.

Energy 436Kcal/1803kJ; Protein 21.5g; Carbohydrate 12.6g, of which sugars 7.5g; Fat 33.3g, of which saturates 5.1g; Cholesterol 285mg; Calcium 464mg; Fibre 7.3g; Sodium 428mg.

BROAD BEAN SALAD AND CARROT SALAD

THESE TWO SALADS ARE FREQUENTLY SERVED TOGETHER. THE FLAVOURS ARE COMPLEMENTARY, AND THE INTENSE GREEN OF THE SHELLED BROAD BEANS PROVIDES A PERFECT CONTRAST TO THE ORANGE OF THE CARROTS. THESE PARTICULAR RECIPES COME FROM MOROCCO, AS IS INDICATED BY THE PRESERVED LEMON IN THE BEAN MIXTURE.

SERVES FOUR

INGREDIENTS

For the broad bean salad
  2kg/4½lb broad (fava) beans
  60–75ml/4–5 tbsp olive oil
  juice of ½ lemon
  2 garlic cloves, finely chopped
  5ml/1 tsp ground cumin
  10ml/2 tsp paprika
  small bunch of coriander (cilantro),
  1 preserved lemon, chopped
  salt and ground black pepper
  handful of black olives, to garnish
For the carrot salad
  450g/1lb carrots, cut into sticks
  30–45ml/2–3 tbsp olive oil
  juice of 1 lemon
  2–3 garlic cloves, crushed
  10ml/2 tsp granulated sugar
  5–10ml/1–2 tsp cumin seeds, roasted
  5ml/1 tsp ground cinnamon
  5ml/1 tsp paprika
  small bunch of coriander (cilantro)
  small bunch of mint

1 To make the broad bean salad, bring a large pan of salted water to the boil. Meanwhile, pod the beans. Put the beans in the pan and boil for about 2 minutes, then drain and refresh the beans under cold running water. Drain. Slip off and discard the thick outer skin.

2 Put the beans in a heavy pan and add the olive oil, lemon juice, garlic, cumin and paprika. Cook the beans gently over a low heat for about 10 minutes, then season to taste with salt and pepper and leave to cool in the pan.

3 Tip the beans into a serving bowl, scraping all the juices from the pan. Chop the coriander and add to the beans with the preserved lemon and garnish with the black olives.

COOK'S TIP
To roast cumin seeds, stir them in a heavy pan over a low heat, until they emit a warm, nutty aroma.

4 To make the carrot salad, steam the carrots over a pan of boiling water for about 15 minutes, until tender. While they are still warm, toss the carrots in a serving bowl with the olive oil, lemon juice, garlic and sugar. Season to taste, then add the cumin seeds, cinnamon and paprika.

5 Finally, chop the coriander and mint, and toss with the carrots. Serve warm or at room temperature.

Energy 299Kcal/1247kJ; Protein 11.1g; Carbohydrate 25.1g, of which sugars 11.4g; Fat 17.8g, of which saturates 2.6g; Cholesterol 0mg; Calcium 136mg; Fibre 11.8g; Sodium 44mg.

ZAHLOUK AND PALE COURGETTE AND CAULIFLOWER SALAD

IN MOROCCO, WHERE THESE RECIPES ORIGINATED, COOKS LIKE TO USE ARGAN OIL FOR SPECIAL DRESSINGS. THIS RARE OIL HAS A REDDISH TINGE AND A RICH, NUTTY FLAVOUR.

SERVES FOUR

INGREDIENTS

For the zahlouk
    3 large aubergines (eggplant)
    3–4 large tomatoes
    5ml/1 tsp granulated sugar
    3–4 garlic cloves, crushed
    60ml/4 tbsp olive oil or argan oil
    juice of 1 lemon
    scant 5ml/1 tsp harissa
    5ml/1 tsp cumin seeds, roasted
     and ground
    small bunch of fresh flat leaf parsley
    salt
For the courgette and cauliflower salad
    60ml/4 tbsp olive oil
    2–3 small courgettes (zucchini),
    1 cauliflower, broken into florets
    juice of 1 lemon
    2–3 garlic cloves, crushed
    small bunch of parsley
    salt and ground black pepper
    5ml/1 tsp paprika, to garnish

1 To make the zahlouk, peel and cube the aubergines and boil in a pan of plenty of salted water for about 15 minutes, until they are very soft. Drain and squeeze out the excess water, then chop and mash them with a fork.

2 Skin and chop the tomatoes. Put the pulped tomatoes in a pan, stir in the sugar, and cook over a gentle heat, until they are reduced to a thick sauce.

3 Add the mashed aubergines. Stir in the garlic, olive or argan oil, lemon juice, harissa and ground cumin. Chop the parsley and add to the aubergine mix, stir until well mixed. Season with salt to taste.

4 To make the courgette and cauliflower salad, thickly slice the courgettes, then heat about half of the olive oil in a heavy pan and brown the courgettes on both sides. Drain on kitchen paper.

5 Meanwhile, steam the cauliflower over a pan of boiling water for 7–10 minutes, until tender. While the cauliflower is still warm, mash it lightly in a bowl and mix in the remaining olive oil, half the lemon juice and the garlic. Add the courgettes. Finely chop the parsley, and add to the salad together with the remaining lemon juice. Season with salt and pepper.

6 Serve the zahlouk at room temperature with plenty of flat bread. Serve the courgette and cauliflower salad sprinkled with paprika.

Energy 302Kcal/1251kJ; Protein 8.3g; Carbohydrate 12.5g, of which sugars 11.5g; Fat 24.7g, of which saturates 3.7g; Cholesterol 0mg; Calcium 139mg; Fibre 8.6g; Sodium 37mg.

GARI FOTO

THE NAME SUGGESTS THIS DISH MIGHT INSPIRE GUESTS TO GET OUT THEIR CAMERAS. IT IS A WEST AFRICAN SPECIALITY, THICKENED WITH A COARSE GROUND FLOUR MADE FROM GROUND CASSAVA ROOT.

SERVES FOUR

INGREDIENTS
25g/1oz/2 tbsp butter or margarine
1 onion, chopped
3 tomatoes, skinned and chopped
15ml/1 tbsp tomato purée (paste)
175g/6oz carrots, chopped
115g/4oz/⅔ cup corn
175g/6oz red (bell) peppers, seeded
  and chopped
300ml/½ pint/1¼ cups vegetable
  stock or water
1 fresh green chilli, seeded
  and chopped
115g/4oz gari

COOK'S TIP
Gari, used in many African recipes, is a coarse flour made from cassava.

1 Melt the butter or margarine in a non-stick pan and fry the onion and tomatoes until pulpy, stirring frequently.

2 Add the tomato purée and carrots and fry for a few minutes, then stir in the corn, red peppers, stock or water and chilli. Bring to the boil, and then cover and simmer for 5 minutes.

3 Slowly mix the gari into the sauce, stirring constantly, until it is well mixed with the vegetables.

4 Cover the pan and cook over a low heat for 5–8 minutes. Transfer the mixture to a serving dish and serve hot.

FUFU

EVERY AFRICAN COUNTRY HAS A VERSION OF THIS PORRIDGE-LIKE SIDE DISH, DESIGNED TO MOP UP THE LIQUID FROM A STEW. IN SOUTHERN AFRICA IT IS CALLED PUTU AND IS MADE WITH CORN MEAL. WEST AFRICANS PREFER TO USE GROUND RICE, SOMETIMES WITH SEMOLINA.

SERVES FOUR

INGREDIENTS
300ml/½ pint/1¼ cups milk
300ml/½ pint/1¼ cups water
25g/1oz/2 tbsp butter
  or margarine
2.5ml/½ tsp salt
15ml/1 tbsp chopped
  fresh parsley
275g/10oz/1½ cups ground rice

COOK'S TIP
Ground rice is creamy white and when cooked it has a slightly grainy texture. Although often used in sweet dishes, it is a tasty grain to serve with savoury dishes too. The addition of milk makes it creamier, but it can be replaced with water, if preferred.

1 Place the milk, water and butter or margarine and salt in a pan, bring to the boil and then turn the heat to low.

2 Add the chopped parsley. Then gradually add the ground rice, stirring vigorously with a wooden spoon to prevent the rice becoming lumpy.

3 Cover the pan and cook over a low heat for about 15 minutes, beating the mixture regularly every 2 minutes to prevent lumps forming.

4 To test if the rice is cooked, rub a pinch of the mixture between your fingers; if it feels smooth and fairly dry, it is ready; if not, continue cooking for a few more minutes and then test again. Serve hot.

TOP Energy 211Kcal/880kJ; Protein 4.6g; Carbohydrate 33.1g, of which sugars 10.9g; Fat 6.7g, of which saturates 3.4g; Cholesterol 13mg; Calcium 32mg; Fibre 3.8g; Sodium 68mg.
BOTTOM Energy 319Kcal/1333kJ; Protein 7.1g; Carbohydrate 56.9g, of which sugars 3.6g; Fat 7.2g, of which saturates 4.1g; Cholesterol 18mg; Calcium 105mg; Fibre 0g; Sodium 316mg.

TANZANIAN VEGETABLE RICE

KERNELS OF CORN AND SMALL PIECES OF CARROT AND PEPPER MAKE THIS A COLOURFUL ACCOMPANIMENT. IT TASTES GREAT WITH GRILLED OR BAKED CHICKEN. IN TANZANIA THE RICE IS OFTEN SERVED WITH A DELICIOUS FRESH RELISH CALLED KACHUMBALI.

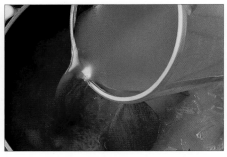

4 Add the garlic and the stock or water and stir well. Bring to the boil and cook over a high heat for 5 minutes, then reduce the heat, cover and cook the rice for 20 minutes.

5 Scatter the corn over the rice, then scatter the pepper on top and lastly sprinkle over the grated carrot.

SERVES FOUR

INGREDIENTS
    350g/12oz/1¾ cups basmati rice
    45ml/3 tbsp vegetable oil
    1 onion, chopped
    2 garlic cloves, crushed
    750ml/1¼ pints/3 cups vegetable
      stock or water
    115g/4oz/⅔ cup corn
    ½ red or green (bell) pepper,
      chopped
    1 large carrot, grated

2 Heat the oil in a large pan and fry the onion for a few minutes over a medium heat, until just soft.

1 Wash the rice in a sieve under cold running water, then leave to drain for about 15 minutes.

3 Add the rice and stir-fry for about 10 minutes, taking care to keep stirring all the time so that the rice doesn't stick to the pan.

6 Cover tightly and steam over a low heat until the rice is cooked, then mix the ingredients together with a fork and serve immediately.

Energy 455Kcal/1902kJ; Protein 8.3g; Carbohydrate 84.2g, of which sugars 8.5g; Fat 9.3g, of which saturates 1.1g; Cholesterol 0mg; Calcium 34mg; Fibre 1.9g; Sodium 84mg.

MOROCCAN BREAD

WARM THIS BREAD IN THE OVEN AND CUT IT INTO THICK SLICES TO SERVE WITH ANY CLASSIC MOROCCAN SAVOURY DISH. IT TASTES GOOD WITH A TAGINE, BUT IS EVEN BETTER WITH A STEW THAT HAS PLENTY OF LIQUID. USE IT TO MOP UP EVERY MORSEL OF SAUCE.

MAKES TWO LOAVES

INGREDIENTS
275g/10oz/2½ cups strong white
  bread flour
175g/6oz/1½ cups wholemeal
  (whole-wheat) flour
10ml/2 tsp salt
about 250ml/8fl oz/1 cup warm milk
  and water mixed
10ml/2 tsp sesame seeds
For the yeast starter
150ml/¼ pint/⅔ cup warm milk and
  water mixed
5ml/1 tsp granulated sugar
10ml/2 tsp dried yeast

1 First prepare the yeast. Place the warm milk mixture in a small bowl or jug (pitcher), stir in the sugar and then sprinkle with the yeast. Stir, then set aside in a warm place for about 10 minutes, until the yeast is frothy.

2 In a bowl, mix together the two flours and salt. Add the yeast mixture and enough warm milk and water to make a soft dough. Knead into a ball and then knead on a floured surface for 10 minutes.

3 Divide the dough into two equal pieces and shape into flattened ball shapes. Place on floured baking trays and press down with your hand to make round breads about 13–15cm/5–6in in diameter.

4 Cover the breads with oiled clear film (plastic wrap) or a clean, damp cloth and set aside in a warm place for 1–1½ hours, until risen. The breads are ready to bake when the dough springs back if gently pressed with a finger.

5 Preheat the oven to 200°C/400°F/ Gas 6. Sprinkle the loaves with the sesame seeds and bake in the oven for 12 minutes. Reduce the heat to 150°C/300°F/Gas 2 and continue baking for 20–30 minutes, until they are golden brown and sound hollow when tapped underneath. Serve warm.

Energy 770Kcal/3271kJ; Protein 25g; Carbohydrate 162.8g, of which sugars 3.9g; Fat 6.6g, of which saturates 1g; Cholesterol 0mg; Calcium 260mg; Fibre 12.6g; Sodium 1973mg.

PASTRIES
AND DESSERTS

Filled with fresh fruit or nuts, then fashioned into elaborate

shapes, the pastries emerge from the oven to be coated in syrup or

honey. Family meals usually conclude in Africa with fresh fruit.

Sherbet is often served, or there may be a fragrant rice pudding.

Sweet treats like Ghoriba and briouates are a popular snack

to enjoy with coffee or tea.

KAAB ᴇʟ GHZAL

BETTER KNOWN BY THEIR FRENCH NAME OF CORNES DE GAZELLES — GAZELLE HORNS — THESE CURVED PASTRIES FILLED WITH ORANGE-SCENTED ALMOND PASTE ARE ONE OF MOROCCO'S FAVOURITE SWEET TREATS. THEY ARE TRADITIONALLY SERVED AT WEDDINGS.

4 Preheat the oven to 180°C/350°F/Gas 4. Take small pieces of the almond paste and roll them between your hands into thin "sausages" about 7.5cm/3in long with tapering ends.

5 Place these in a line along one side of the strips of pastry, about 3cm/1¼in apart. Dampen the pastry edges with water and then fold the other half of the strip over the filling and press the edges together firmly to seal.

MAKES ABOUT SIXTEEN

INGREDIENTS
   200g/7oz/1¾ cups plain
    (all-purpose) flour
   25g/1oz/2 tbsp butter, melted
   about 30ml/2 tbsp orange flower
    water or water
   1 large egg yolk, beaten
   pinch of salt
   icing (confectioners') sugar, to serve
For the almond paste
   200g/7oz/1 cups ground almonds
   115g/4oz/1¾ cups icing
    (confectioners') sugar or
    caster (superfine) sugar
   30ml/2 tbsp orange flower water
   25g/1oz/2 tbsp butter, melted
   2 egg yolks, beaten
   2.5ml/½ tsp ground cinnamon

1 First make the almond paste. Mix together all the ingredients to make a smooth paste.

2 To make the pastry, mix the flour and a pinch of salt and then stir in the melted butter, orange flower water or water, and about three-quarters of the egg yolk. Stir in enough cold water, little by little, to make a fairly soft dough.

3 Knead the dough for about 10 minutes, until smooth and elastic, then place on a floured surface and roll out as thinly as possible. Cut the dough into long strips about 7.5cm/3in wide.

6 Using a pastry wheel, cut around each "sausage" (as you would with ravioli) to make a crescent shape. Make sure that the edges are firmly pinched together.

7 Prick the crescents with a fork or a needle and place on a buttered baking tray. Brush with the remaining beaten egg yolk and then bake in the oven for 12–16 minutes, until lightly coloured. Remove to a wire rack, cool and then dust with icing sugar. Serve warm or cold.

Energy 163Kcal/682kJ; Protein 4g; Carbohydrate 18.1g, of which sugars 8.2g; Fat 8.8g, of which saturates 1.5g; Cholesterol 16mg; Calcium 53mg; Fibre 1.3g; Sodium 13mg.

BRIOUATES WITH ALMONDS AND DATES

THESE MOROCCAN PASTRIES, MADE WITH FILO OR THE LOCAL EQUIVALENT — OUARKA — ARE A FAVOURITE TREAT. BRIOUATES CAN BE SAVOURY, BUT THESE ARE UNASHAMEDLY SWEET. THE FILLING IS A DATE AND ALMOND PASTE AND THEY ARE COATED IN HONEY AND ORANGE FLOWER WATER.

MAKES ABOUT THIRTY

INGREDIENTS
- 15ml/1 tbsp sunflower oil
- 225g/8oz/1⅓ cups blanched almonds
- 115g/4oz/⅔ cup stoned (pitted) dried dates
- 25g/1oz/2 tbsp butter, softened
- 5ml/1 tsp ground cinnamon
- 1.5ml/¼ tsp almond essence (extract)
- 40g/1½oz/⅓ cup icing (confectioners') sugar
- 30ml/2 tbsp orange flower water or rose water
- 10 sheets of filo pastry
- 50g/2oz/¼ cup butter, melted
- 120ml/4fl oz/½ cup clear honey
- dates, to serve (optional)

4 Place a walnut-size piece of almond paste at the bottom of each strip. Fold one corner over the filling to make a triangle and then fold up, in triangles, to make a neat packet.

5 Brush the filo packet again with a little melted butter and set aside. Repeat steps 3 and 4 to make around 30 pastries.

6 While the briouates are cooking, pour the honey and a little orange flower or rose water into a pan and heat very gently. When the pastries are cooked, lower them one by one into the pan and turn them in the honey so that they are thoroughly coated all over.

7 Transfer the briouates to a plate and cool a little before serving, with dates if you wish.

1 Heat the oil in a small pan and fry the almonds for a few minutes until golden, stirring all the time. Drain on kitchen paper to cool, then grind the almonds in a coffee or spice mill. Process the dates in a blender or food processor.

2 Spoon the ground almonds into a mixing bowl or into the blender or food processor with the dates, and blend with the softened butter, cinnamon, almond essence, icing sugar and a little flower water to taste. If the mixture feels stiff, work in extra flower water.

3 Preheat the oven to 180°C/350°F/ Gas 4. Brush a sheet of filo pastry with melted butter and cut into three equal strips, keeping the remaining sheets covered with clear film (plastic wrap) to prevent them drying out.

Energy 95Kcal/396kJ; Protein 1.8g; Carbohydrate 7.5g, of which sugars 6g; Fat 6.6g, of which saturates 1.7g; Cholesterol 5mg; Calcium 23mg; Fibre 0.7g; Sodium 17mg.

GHORIBA

CRISP ON THE OUTSIDE, BUT MELTINGLY SOFT IN THE MIDDLE, THESE MOROCCAN ALMOND BISCUITS ARE A POPULAR MID-MORNING SNACK WITH COFFEE OR TEA.

MAKES ABOUT THIRTY

INGREDIENTS
   2 egg yolks
   1 egg white
   200g/7oz/1¾ cups icing
      (confectioners') sugar, plus extra
      for dusting
   10ml/2 tsp baking powder
   finely grated rind of ½ lemon
   a few drops of vanilla
      essence (extract)
   about 350g/12oz/3 cups
      ground almonds
   sunflower oil, for greasing

VARIATION
Use ground hazelnuts instead of
ground almonds.

1 Preheat the oven to 180°C/350°F/
Gas 4. In a bowl, beat together the egg
yolks and egg white with the icing
sugar. Add the baking powder, lemon
rind and vanilla essence, with enough
of the ground almonds to make a stiff
paste. Knead the mixture together with
your hands. Oil your hands with
sunflower oil.

2 Take walnut-size pieces of paste and
roll into small balls. Flatten on a board
dusted with icing sugar and then place
on a greased baking tray about
4cm/1½in apart. Bake for 15 minutes,
until golden. Cool on a wire rack.

HONEYCOMB PANCAKES

LIKE DROP SCONES, THESE POPULAR PANCAKES BUBBLE WHEN THE BATTER IS SPOONED INTO A PAN, ACQUIRING A HONEYCOMB TEXTURE. ALSO KNOWN AS BEGHRIR, THEY ARE DELICIOUS WITH BUTTER AND HONEY AND ARE TRADITIONALLY EATEN AFTER SUNSET DURING RAMADAN.

MAKES ABOUT TWELVE

INGREDIENTS
   175g/6oz/1½ cups self-raising
      (self-rising) flour
   10ml/2 tsp baking powder
   30ml/2 tbsp caster (superfine) sugar
   1 egg
   175ml/6fl oz/¾ cup semi-skimmed
      (low-fat) milk
   15ml/1 tbsp rose water or orange
      flower water
   15ml/1 tbsp melted butter
   sunflower oil, for greasing

COOK'S TIP
Serve these pancakes warm and topped
with a knob (pat) of butter on each one.
For a breakfast treat, serve with melted
butter and a generous helping of real
maple syrup.

1 Mix together the flour, baking powder
and sugar in a bowl. Add the egg and
milk and blend to make a thick batter.
Stir in the rose or orange flower water
and then beat in the melted butter.

2 Heat a frying pan and brush the
surface with a little oil. Pour in a small
ladleful of batter, smoothing with the
back of a spoon to make a round about
10cm/4in across. Cook for a few
minutes until bubbles appear on the
surface, then place on a large plate.

3 Cook the remaining pancakes in the
same way and place them on the plate
in overlapping circles to make a
honeycomb pattern. Serve warm.

TOP Energy 102Kcal/426kJ; Protein 2.8g; Carbohydrate 7.8g, of which sugars 7.5g; Fat 6.9g, of which saturates 0.6g; Cholesterol 13mg; Calcium 33mg; Fibre 0.9g; Sodium 5mg.
BOTTOM Energy 82Kcal/346kJ; Protein 2.4g; Carbohydrate 14.6g, of which sugars 3.5g; Fat 1.9g, of which saturates 1g; Cholesterol 19mg; Calcium 42mg; Fibre 0.5g; Sodium 20mg.

TROPICAL FRUIT PANCAKES

IN THIS SOUTH AFRICAN DESSERT, PANCAKES ARE FILLED WITH A MIXTURE OF MANGOES, BANANAS, KIWI FRUIT AND ORANGES, MOISTENED WITH A HONEYED CITRUS SYRUP FLAVOURED WITH VAN DER HUM, THE LOCAL BRANDY-BASED TANGERINE LIQUEUR.

SERVES FOUR

INGREDIENTS
   115g/4oz/1 cup self-raising
     (self-rising) flour
   pinch of freshly grated nutmeg
   15ml/1 tbsp caster (superfine) sugar
   1 egg
   300ml/½ pint/1¼ cups milk
   15ml/1 tbsp melted butter or
     margarine, plus extra for frying
   15ml/1 tbsp fine desiccated
     (dry unsweetened shredded)
     coconut (optional)
   whipped fresh cream, to serve
For the filling
   225g/8oz prepared ripe, firm mango
   2 bananas
   2 kiwi fruit
   1 large orange
   15ml/1 tbsp lemon juice
   30ml/2 tbsp orange juice
   15ml/1 tbsp clear honey
   30–45ml/2–3 tbsp orange liqueur
     (optional)

1 Sift the flour, nutmeg and caster sugar into a large bowl, add the egg and most of the milk and beat with a wooden spoon to make a thick, smooth batter.

2 Add the remaining milk, melted butter or margarine, and the coconut, if using, and continue beating until the batter is smooth and of a fairly thin, dropping consistency.

3 Melt a little butter or margarine in a large non-stick frying pan.

4 Swirl the hot fat round the pan then pour in a little batter to cover the base. Fry until golden, then toss or turn with a spatula. Repeat with the remaining mixture to make about eight pancakes.

5 Dice the mango, roughly chop the bananas and slice the kiwi fruit. Cut away the peel and pith from the orange and cut into segments.

6 Place the fruit in a bowl. Mix together the lemon and orange juices, honey and orange liqueur, if using, then pour over the fruit. Fold a pancake in half and spoon a little of the fruit in the centre, Fold the corners over. Serve with whipped cream.

Energy 303Kcal/1285kJ; Protein 8.5g; Carbohydrate 56.5g, of which sugars 34g; Fat 6.5g, of which saturates 3.3g; Cholesterol 60mg; Calcium 239mg; Fibre 4.1g; Sodium 182mg.

MINTED POMEGRANATE YOGURT
WITH GRAPEFRUIT SALAD

RUBY RED OR SALMON PINK, THE JEWEL-LIKE SEEDS OF THE POMEGRANATE MAKE ANY DESSERT LOOK
BEAUTIFUL. HERE THEY ARE STIRRED INTO YOGURT TO MAKE A DELICATE SAUCE FOR A FRESH-TASTING
GRAPEFRUIT SALAD. THE FLECKS OF GREEN ARE FINELY CHOPPED FRESH MINT, WHICH COMPLEMENT
THE CITRUS FLAVOURS PERFECTLY. SERVE THE COMBINATION FOR BREAKFAST, AS A LIGHT SNACK
DURING THE DAY, OR AS A DESSERT AFTER A SPICY MAIN COURSE.

SERVES THREE TO FOUR

INGREDIENTS
    300ml/½ pint/1¼ cups Greek
        (US strained plain) yogurt
    2–3 ripe pomegranates
    small bunch of fresh mint,
        finely chopped
    clear honey or caster (superfine)
        sugar, to taste (optional)
For the grapefruit salad
    2 red grapefruits
    2 pink grapefruits
    1 white grapefruit
    15–30ml/1–2 tbsp orange
        flower water
To decorate
    handful of pomegranate seeds
    fresh mint leaves

1 Put the yogurt in a bowl and beat well. Cut open the pomegranates and scoop out the seeds, removing and discarding all the bitter pith. Fold the pomegranate seeds and chopped mint into the yogurt. Sweeten with a little honey or sugar, if using, then chill until ready to serve.

2 Peel the red, pink and white grapefruits, cutting off and discarding all the pith. Cut between the membranes to remove the segments, holding the fruit over a bowl to catch the juices.

3 Discard the membranes and mix the fruit segments with the reserved juices. Sprinkle with the orange flower water and add a little honey or sugar, if using. Stir gently then decorate with a few pomegranate seeds.

4 Decorate the chilled yogurt with a sprinkling of pomegranate seeds and mint leaves, and serve with the grapefruit salad.

VARIATION
Alternatively, you can use a mixture of oranges and blood oranges, interspersed with thin segments of lemon. Lime segments work well with the grapefruit and mandarins or tangerines could be used too. As the idea is to create a refreshing, scented salad, juicy melons and kiwi fruit would also be ideal.

Energy 188Kcal/784kJ; Protein 8.8g; Carbohydrate 18g, of which sugars 18g; Fat 10.5g, of which saturates 5.2g; Cholesterol 0mg; Calcium 202mg; Fibre 3.6g; Sodium 82mg.

ALMOND MILK

ALMOND MILK HAS BEEN A FAVOURITE BEVERAGE SINCE MEDIEVAL TIMES, WHEN IT WAS VALUED BECAUSE IT COULD BE MADE AS NEEDED, AND DID NOT SOUR LIKE THE DAIRY PRODUCT. IT IS POPULAR THROUGHOUT NORTH AFRICA, WHICH IS WHERE THIS VERSION COMES FROM. THE ADDITION OF ORANGE FLOWER WATER IS A MOROCCAN REFINEMENT. THE DRINK SHOULD BE SERVED VERY COLD, PREFERABLY IN GLASSES THAT HAVE BEEN FROSTED BY BEING PLACED IN THE FREEZER.

SERVES EIGHT TO TEN

INGREDIENTS
  500g/1¼lb/generous 2¾ cups
    blanched almonds
  1.2 litres/2 pints/5 cups water
  200g/7oz/1 cup caster
    (superfine) sugar
  15ml/1 tbsp orange flower water

VARIATION
Use blanched hazelnuts instead
of almonds if you like.

1 Using a mortar and pestle or a blender, reduce the almonds to a smooth paste. Adding a splash of water will help to make the paste smoother. Put the water and sugar in a large pan and bring to the boil, stirring until the sugar has dissolved. Stir in the almond paste and simmer for 5 minutes.

2 Turn off the heat and stir in the orange flower water. Leave the mixture to cool in the pan so that the flavours mingle, then strain through muslin (cheesecloth) or a fine sieve. Pour the strained milk into glasses and chill thoroughly in the freezer, so that it is almost setting into ice when served.

Energy 48Kcal/198kJ; Protein 4.4g; Carbohydrate 1.2g, of which sugars 1.2g; Fat 2.4g, of which saturates 0.5g; Cholesterol 0mg; Calcium 20mg; Fibre 0g; Sodium 48mg.

ALMOND AND PISTACHIO ICE CREAMS

SIT AT A PAVEMENT CAFÉ IN CAIRO AND YOU CAN SAMPLE SOME OF THE MOST DELICIOUS ICE CREAMS IN THE WORLD. THERE'S KEEN DEBATE ABOUT WHICH TASTES THE BEST. COOL GREEN PISTACHIO AND SNOWY ALMOND COME HIGH ON THE LIST, ALONG WITH DELICATE ROSE WATER ICE CREAM AND VIBRANT, NOT-TO-BE-MISSED MANGO. ALTHOUGH PISTACHIO AND ALMOND ARE BOTH NUT ICES, THEIR FLAVOURS ARE MARKEDLY DIFFERENT, AND WHEN PRESENTED TOGETHER, THEY ARE SENSATIONAL.

SERVES FOUR

INGREDIENTS
For the almond ice cream
    150g/5oz/1¼ cups blanched
      almonds, finely ground
    300ml/½ pint/1¼ cups milk
    300ml/½ pint/1¼ cups double
      (heavy) cream
    4 egg yolks
    175g/6oz/generous ¾ cup caster
      (superfine) sugar
    30–45ml/2–3 tbsp orange
      flower water
    2–3 drops almond essence (extract)
For the pistachio ice cream
    150g/5oz/1¼ cups pistachio nuts,
      blanched and finely ground
    300ml/½ pint/1¼ cups milk
    300ml/½ pint/1¼ cups double
      (heavy) cream
    4 egg yolks
    175g/6oz/generous ¾ cup caster
      (superfine) sugar
    30–45ml/2–3 tbsp rose water
    green food colouring (optional)

1 To make the almond ice cream, put the almonds in a pan with the milk and cream, and bring to the boil. In a large bowl, beat the egg yolks with the sugar, then pour in the hot milk and cream, beating all the time. Pour the mixture back into the pan and stir over a low heat, until it thickens slightly. Do not overheat the custard as, if it approaches simmering point, it will curdle.

2 Stir in the orange flower water and almond essence, and then leave the mixture to cool. Pour the cold mixture into a bowl or freezerproof container and chill, then freeze. Whisk the mixture thoroughly after about 1 hour, when it should be icy around the edges.

3 Continue to freeze the ice cream, whisking it two or three more times, until it is smooth and very thick. Return it to the freezer and leave for several hours or overnight. Alternatively, churn the mixture in an ice cream maker.

4 Make the pistachio ice cream in the same way as the almond ice cream, using the pistachio nuts in place of the almonds and rose water instead of the orange flower water and almond essence. Add a little green food colouring to the pistachio ice cream, if you like.

5 Remove both batches of ice cream from the freezer 10–15 minutes before serving and allow it to soften slightly.

Energy 1735Kcal/7212kJ; Protein 28.4g; Carbohydrate 106.7g, of which sugars 104.8g; Fat 135.8g, of which saturates 59.3g; Cholesterol 618mg; Calcium 478mg; Fibre 5.1g; Sodium 325mg.

BANANA AND MELON IN ORANGE VANILLA SAUCE

THE INDIAN OCEAN ISLAND OF MADAGASCAR IS A MAJOR PRODUCER OF VANILLA, SO IT IS NOT SURPRISING TO FIND THE SPICE FLAVOURING THIS DESSERT FROM NEIGHBOURING MOZAMBIQUE.

SERVES FOUR

INGREDIENTS
300ml/½ pint/1¼ cups orange juice
1 vanilla pod (bean) or a few drops of
  vanilla essence (extract)
5ml/1 tsp finely grated orange rind
15ml/1 tbsp granulated sugar
4 bananas
1 honeydew melon
30ml/2 tbsp lemon juice

1 Place the orange juice in a small pan with the vanilla pod or vanilla essence, orange rind and sugar and bring gently to the boil.

2 Reduce the heat and simmer gently for 15 minutes, until the sauce is syrupy. Remove from the heat and leave to cool. Once cool, remove and discard the vanilla pod, if using.

3 Peel and roughly chop the bananas and peel, seed and roughly chop the melon. Place the chopped bananas and melon in a large serving bowl and toss with the lemon juice.

COOK'S TIPS
To check whether a melon is ripe, lightly press the area around the centre of the tip of the melon, the surface should give slightly. A ripe melon will also smell pleasantly sweet.

4 Pour the cooled sauce over the fruit and chill in the refrigerator for at least 1 hour before serving.

BANANA MANDAZI

VERSIONS OF THIS MUCH-LOVED DESSERT — BANANA FRITTERS — ARE FOUND THROUGHOUT AFRICA, FROM KENYA TO KWAZULU-NATAL, IN ZAÏRE AND IN THE WEST AND NORTH OF THE CONTINENT.

SERVES FOUR

INGREDIENTS
1 egg
2 ripe bananas, roughly chopped
150ml/¼ pint/⅔ cup milk
2.5ml/½ tsp vanilla essence (extract)
225g/8oz/2 cups self-raising
  (self-rising) flour
5ml/1 tsp baking powder
45ml/3 tbsp caster (superfine) sugar
vegetable oil, for deep-frying

1 Place the egg, bananas, milk, vanilla essence, flour, baking powder and sugar in a blender or food processor.

2 Process to make a smooth batter. It should have a creamy dropping consistency. If it is too thick, add a little extra milk. Set aside for 10 minutes.

3 Heat the oil in a heavy pan or deep-fryer. When hot, carefully place spoonfuls of the mixture in the oil and deep-fry for 3–4 minutes, until golden. Remove with a slotted spoon and drain on kitchen paper. Keep warm while cooking the remaining mandazis, then serve at once.

TOP Energy 158Kcal/662kJ; Protein 2.3g; Carbohydrate 37.9g, of which sugars 35.6g; Fat 0.6g, of which saturates 0.1g; Cholesterol 0mg; Calcium 25mg; Fibre 1.9g; Sodium 48mg.
BOTTOM Energy 387Kcal/1637kJ; Protein 8.5g; Carbohydrate 67.7g, of which sugars 24.7g; Fat 11.1g, of which saturates 1.9g; Cholesterol 50mg; Calcium 258mg; Fibre 2.3g; Sodium 237mg.

FRESH PINEAPPLE <u>WITH</u> COCONUT

IN THOSE PARTS OF AFRICA WHERE PINEAPPLES ARE GROWN, THE FRUIT AND THE FRESHLY PRESSED
JUICE ARE SOLD AT ROADSIDE STALLS. THIS RECIPE CELEBRATES THE FRUIT'S FANTASTIC FLAVOUR.

SERVES FOUR

INGREDIENTS
  1 fresh pineapple, peeled
  slivers of fresh coconut
  300ml/½ pint/1¼ cups
    pineapple juice
  60ml/4 tbsp coconut liqueur
  2.5cm/1in piece of preserved stem
    ginger, plus 45ml/3 tbsp of
    the syrup

1 Slice the pineapple, arrange in a serving dish and scatter the coconut slivers on top.

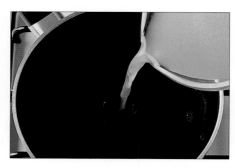

2 Place the pineapple juice and coconut liqueur in a pan and heat gently.

3 Thinly slice the preserved stem ginger and add to the pan together with the ginger syrup. Bring just to the boil and then simmer gently, until the liquid is slightly reduced and the sauce is fairly thick.

4 Pour the sauce over the pineapple and coconut, leave to cool, then chill in the refrigerator before serving.

VARIATION
If fresh coconut is not available, then use desiccated (dry unsweetened shredded) coconut instead.

Energy 175Kcal/744kJ; Protein 1.2g; Carbohydrate 31.9g, of which sugars 31.9g; Fat 2g, of which saturates 1.3g; Cholesterol 0mg; Calcium 43mg; Fibre 2.8g; Sodium 12mg.

EGYPTIAN BREAD AND BUTTER PUDDING

THIS PUDDING IS RATHER ODDLY NAMED, SINCE IT CONTAINS NEITHER BREAD NOR BUTTER. WHAT IT HAS IN COMMON WITH THE CLASSIC ENGLISH DISH IS THE CUSTARD, WHICH IS POURED OVER LAYERS OF FINE PASTRY OR CRACKERS. THE LOCAL NAME IS OMM'ALI, WHICH MEANS "MOTHER OF ALI".

SERVES FOUR

INGREDIENTS
10–12 sheets of filo pastry
600ml/1 pint/2½ cups milk
250ml/8fl oz/1 cup double
  (heavy) cream
1 egg, beaten
30ml/2 tbsp rose water
50g/2oz/½ cup each chopped
  pistachio nuts, almonds and
  hazelnuts
115g/4oz/¾ cup raisins
15ml/1 tbsp ground cinnamon
single (light) cream, to serve

1 Preheat the oven to 160°C/325°F/Gas 3. Lay the filo pastry sheets on top of each other on a baking sheet and bake in the oven for 15–20 minutes until crisp. Remove from the oven and increase the heat to 200°C/400°F/Gas 6.

2 Scald the milk and cream by pouring them into a pan and heating very gently, until hot but not boiling. Slowly add the beaten egg and the rose water. Cook over a low heat, until it thickens, stirring all the time. Remove from the heat.

3 Crumble the pastry using your hands and then spread it in layers with the nuts and raisins in the base of a greased shallow baking dish.

4 Pour the custard mixture evenly over the nut and pastry base and then bake in the oven for 20 minutes, until golden. Sprinkle with cinnamon and serve with single cream.

Energy 575Kcal/2393kJ; Protein 10.1g; Carbohydrate 38.8g, of which sugars 28.9g; Fat 43.3g, of which saturates 23.4g; Cholesterol 95mg; Calcium 255mg; Fibre 1.7g; Sodium 162mg.

Figs and Pears in Honey

Fresh figs picked straight from the tree are so delicious that it seems almost sacrilege to cook them — unless of course, you try this superb method.

SERVES FOUR

INGREDIENTS
1 lemon
90ml/6 tbsp clear honey
1 cinnamon stick
1 cardamom pod
350ml/12fl oz/1½ cups water
2 pears
8 fresh figs, halved

1 Pare the rind from the lemon using a zester or vegetable peeler and cut the rind into very thin strips.

2 Place the lemon rind, honey, cinnamon stick, cardamom pod and the water in a pan and boil, uncovered, for about 10 minutes, until the liquid is reduced by about half.

3 Cut the pears into eighths, discarding the core. Leave the peel on or discard, as preferred. Place in the syrup, add the figs and simmer for about 5 minutes, until the fruit is tender.

4 Transfer the fruit to a serving bowl with a slotted spoon. Cook the liquid until syrupy, discard the cinnamon stick and pour over the figs and pears. Serve.

Moroccan-style Plum Pudding

There's a strong French influence in Moroccan cooking, as evidenced by this North African version of the batter pudding known as clafouti. Ground rice and flaked almonds thicken the milk mixture, which is flavoured with orange flower water.

SERVES FOUR

INGREDIENTS
450g/1lb fresh plums or other fruit
   (see Variation)
600ml/1 pint/2½ cups skimmed or
   semi-skimmed (low-fat) milk
45ml/3 tbsp ground rice
30–45ml/2–3 tbsp caster
   (superfine) sugar
75g/3oz/¾ cup flaked almonds
30ml/2 tbsp orange flower water or
   rose water, to taste
icing (confectioners') sugar,
   to decorate

1 Preheat the oven to 190°C/375°F/ Gas 5. Stone (pit) and halve the plums. Bring the milk to the boil in a pan.

2 Blend the ground rice with 30–45ml/ 2–3 tbsp cold water, beating well to remove lumps. Pour the hot milk over the rice then pour back into the pan. Simmer over a low heat for 5 minutes, until it thickens, stirring all the time.

3 Add the caster sugar and flaked almonds and cook gently for a further 5 minutes. Stir in the orange flower or rose water and simmer for 2 minutes.

4 Butter a shallow ovenproof dish and pour in the almond milk mixture. Arrange the prepared fruit on top and then bake in the oven for about 25–30 minutes, until the fruit has softened. Dust with sifted icing sugar and serve.

VARIATION
Apricots, cherries or greengages, can also be used for this pudding.

TOP Energy 186Kcal/790kJ; Protein 1.8g; Carbohydrate 45.9g, of which sugars 45.9g; Fat 0.7g, of which saturates 0g; Cholesterol 0mg; Calcium 110mg; Fibre 4.7g; Sodium 30mg.
BOTTOM Energy 308Kcal/1291kJ; Protein 11g; Carbohydrate 38.1g, of which sugars 28.6g; Fat 13.2g, of which saturates 2.4g; Cholesterol 9mg; Calcium 246mg; Fibre 2.4g; Sodium 69mg.

POACHED PEARS IN SCENTED HONEY SYRUP

FRUIT HAS BEEN POACHED IN HONEY SINCE ANCIENT TIMES. THE ROMANS DID IT, AS DID THE PERSIANS, ARABS, MOORS AND OTTOMANS. THE MOROCCANS CONTINUE THE TRADITION TODAY, ADDING A LITTLE ORANGE RIND OR ANISEED, OR EVEN LAVENDER TO GIVE A SUBTLE FLAVOURING. DELICATE AND PRETTY TO LOOK AT, THESE SCENTED PEARS WOULD PROVIDE AN EXQUISITE FINISHING TOUCH TO ANY MIDDLE EASTERN OR NORTH AFRICAN MEAL.

SERVES FOUR

INGREDIENTS
45ml/3 tbsp clear honey
juice of 1 lemon
250ml/8fl oz/1 cup water
pinch of saffron threads
1 cinnamon stick
2–3 dried lavender heads
4 firm pears

VARIATION
Use whole, peeled nectarines or peaches instead of pears.

1 Heat the honey and lemon juice in a heavy pan that will hold the pears snugly. Stir over a gentle heat until the honey has dissolved. Add the water, saffron threads, cinnamon stick and flowers from 1–2 lavender heads. Bring the mixture to the boil, then reduce the heat and simmer for 5 minutes.

2 Peel the pears, leaving the stalks attached. Add the pears to the pan and simmer for 20 minutes, turning and basting at regular intervals, until they are tender. Leave the pears to cool in the syrup and serve at room temperature, decorated with a few lavender flowers.

Energy 66Kcal/278kJ; Protein 0.5g; Carbohydrate 16.5g, of which sugars 16.5g; Fat 0.2g, of which saturates 0g; Cholesterol 0mg; Calcium 17mg; Fibre 3.3g; Sodium 5mg.

SPICED NUTTY BANANAS

THIS BAKED BANANA DESSERT FROM CENTRAL AFRICA COULDN'T BE SIMPLER. THE NUTTY CRUST CONTRASTS BEAUTIFULLY WITH THE CREAMY BANANA BENEATH, AND THE RUM SAUCE IS DELICIOUS.

SERVES THREE

INGREDIENTS
  6 ripe, but firm, bananas
  30ml/2 tbsp chopped unsalted
    cashew nuts
  30ml/2 tbsp chopped unsalted
    peanuts
  30ml/2 tbsp desiccated (dry
    unsweetened shredded) coconut
  7.5–15ml/½–1 tbsp demerara
    (raw) sugar
  5ml/1 tsp ground cinnamon
  2.5ml/½ tsp freshly grated nutmeg
  150ml/¼ pint/⅔ cup orange juice
  60ml/4 tbsp rum
  15g/½oz/1 tbsp butter or margarine
  double (heavy) cream, to serve

1 Preheat the oven to 200°C/400°F/
Gas 6. Slice the bananas and place them
in a greased, shallow ovenproof dish.

2 Mix together the cashew nuts,
peanuts, coconut, sugar, cinnamon
and nutmeg in a small bowl.

3 Pour the orange juice and rum over
the bananas, then sprinkle the nut and
sugar mixture over the top.

4 Dot the top with butter or margarine,
then bake in the oven for 15–20
minutes, until the bananas are golden
and the sauce is bubbly. Serve with
double cream.

COOK'S TIPS
Freshly grated nutmeg makes all the
difference to this dish. More rum can be
added, if preferred. Chopped mixed nuts
can be used instead of peanuts.

Energy 455Kcal/1902kJ; Protein 7.7g; Carbohydrate 51.5g, of which sugars 45.3g; Fat 20.6g, of which saturates 10g; Cholesterol 11mg; Calcium 29mg; Fibre 4.4g; Sodium 69mg.

INDEX